D0876316

PIONEERS OF SCIENCE

Unless Idealism holds the pen
They labour in vain who use it.

TO
MY MOTHER
AND TO
MARIA PITT-CHATHAM
THIS VOLUME OF STRUGGLE AND VICTORY
IS DEDICATED

PIONEERS OF SCIENCE

SEVEN PICTURES OF
STRUGGLE AND VICTORY

BY

AMELIA DOROTHY DEFRIES

" Not in matter but in thought, not in possessions or even in attainments, but in ideals, are to be found the seeds of immortality."—SIR JAGADIS CHUNDER BOSE, in *The Voice of Life.*

Essay Index Reprint Series

Originally Published by
GEORGE ROUTLEDGE & SONS, LTD

BOOKS FOR LIBRARIES PRESS
FREEPORT, NEW YORK

Library
I.U.P.
Indiana, Pa.
500.92   D362p
c.1

First Published 1928
Reprinted 1970

STANDARD BOOK NUMBER:
8369-1646-8

LIBRARY OF CONGRESS CATALOG CARD NUMBER:
74-117782

PRINTED IN THE UNITED STATES OF AMERICA

CONTENTS

PART I

THE LIVING, BY WHOSE WISDOM WE PROGRESS

PART II

THE DEAD, BY WHOSE LIGHT WE LIVE

"Certainly there is something beyond the individual that is and the world that is."

H. G. WELLS in *The Open Conspiracy.*

PART I

THE LIVING : BY WHOSE WISDOM WE
PROGRESS

INTRODUCTION

THE CHARACTER OF GENIUS

*" Let the imagination go, guarding it by judgement
and principles, but holding it in and directing it by
experiment."*

FARADAY.

SHALL I write of the living or the dead ?

That question confronts every biographer.
" Why not more biographies of the living ? "
asks Arnold Bennett.

Yet Emil Ludwig, almost at the same
moment, writes : " It is best that the por-
traitist should confine himself to characters
who have died and so, as we say, are finished.
. . . The last picture," he thinks, " that is
made of a man, the death mask, will always
remain the truest." Yet his life of the
Kaiser was written while the man yet lived—
only his career being finished . . . and even
now no one can say what his death mask will
be like.

The truth is that every significant life contains several deaths, for there are crises in
every career, during which the spirit wanes—
although later it should wax again ; while the

influence of the man who has died, if it counts at all, lives on. There are seven phases possible in every life and the passage from one phase to another is a crisis, often frought with pain and bitter struggle. More than once in a career it may seem as though the man was "finished." More than once in a life it may seem as though the outlook was hopeless. At such a crisis Papini wrote his *Huomo Finito*, and, like a modern St. Francis, retired to the solitary heights of the mountains outside Florence, to all worldly appearances a "finished" man. But he rose from the ashes of his former (futuristic) self to write his beautiful *Life of Christ*, telling in modern fashion the old story, for the people of his own day, making it live again.

What is true of the individual is true of the race and the nation. In each there is the complex rhythm of life. The biography of a dead person can be nothing but a documentary portrait: the biographer, if he has real literary genius and psychological insight, can breathe on the composite documents and bring them to life—as Ludwig has done with Napoleon. But no one can say if the portrait is really and fully a true one. The convincing writer, by his research, and painstaking study of facts at his disposal, and by his imagination, makes it appear true : yet the same can be done with a character that has never lived at

INTRODUCTION

all ; indeed Fiction can be made to seem truer even than fact. In each case this is the highest point of literary art. The biographer of the dead has all the documents before him : he can weigh in the balance the man's actions, his written word, his influence upon his contemporaries and see the net result of this upon the world. He can open the dead man's letters and there find his character revealed most intimately.

Or he can, as Ludwig has done with Rembrandt, set before himself all the self-portraits of a man and read from these pictures his very soul. But who is there can say if the interpretation thus reached is accurate ?

If one writes about a living man many of these windows into his mind are not yet open. The law of libel sets its limits upon the writer's imagination—even upon his deductions. Thus, suppose a great man is the victim of some secret vice—can it be told while he lives ? Can a writer endanger a living reputation by suggesting its shortcomings, even if these are known to him ? The law of libel hangs like an axe over his head.

Suppose, on the other hand, that the writer be carried away by enthusiasm for the virtues of his model—may not this very enthusiasm lay him and his subject open to ridicule ? Enthusiasm for the living is not popular. I remember hearing of a critic who wrote en-

3

thusiastically about a painter then unknown, and was rewarded by losing that artist's friendship—for his subject turned on him, crying : " You have made me ridiculous ! " One can damn with faint praise, but even worse, it appears, is too much praise.

Yet without enthusiasm could Boswell, Carlyle, Ludwig, have made their subjects live at all ? It is only those characters, living or dead, who have touched a chord, roused enthusiasm, lighted the imagination, that can be used by any artist as subjects for biography.

Thus it comes that, whether writing of the living or the dead, one can only make vital portraits of those into whom one can project oneself, whose lives one can live in imagination. So that every biographer really is forced to select as models those who mirror a latent part of himself.

For we are composite creatures—many-sided, with latent possibilities, and each person that appeals to us forcibly is in reality a hidden part of ourselves. To make the dead live again in terms of our own day is a great imaginative feat—as great as the invention of a character in fiction : perhaps greater, since the imagination is in chain to the known facts.

To portray the living is also a feat, since the living model eludes us, half the time;—the primitive instinct of the wild animal, to hide, is strong in us all!

* * * * * *

I have, here, chosen to attempt portraits of six scientists and an artist.

Why the artist ? Because Art and Science must not be considered as separated, but as parts of a poetic, even mystic, whole. In the past the artist and the scientist were often to be found in one man. To-day the art in science is as much a part of the nature of science as is the science in art, a part of art. That science has always been a great part of art is clear to anyone who has read the book of Cennino Cennini, that beautiful early Renaissance summary of the technical side of the painter's craft ; while the art that is in science is forever recorded in the Note-books of Leonardo da Vinci, and, now again, in the infinite delicacy of modern experiments. Of my six scientists, three are living and three are dead. As a symbol that the dead live on by the light of their spirit I have chosen two men by whose light, quite literally, *we* are nowadays living ; and one who fused by light the chaos and darkness of mediæval thinking.

My four living scientists are men whose work brings light, in this last sense, to the world, and with very practical results.

5

Yet in themselves all, except one, of the seven are but as other men—simple, unaffected, human, workers and breadwinners.

I feel that a portrait of a living man, though of necessity lacking finality, is likely to be truer (because subject to his own criticism and to that of his friends) than the portrait made after death.

* * * * * *

In the normal course of human life there are seven phases, broadly corresponding to the Olympians of the Greeks, and to the Seven Sacraments ; and these are even found to correspond to the phases of animal life and even to those of the vegetable world.[1]

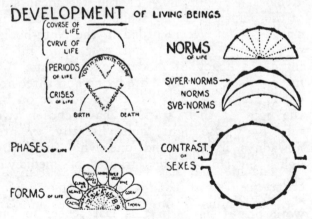

DEVELOPMENT OF LIVING BEINGS

[1] See *The Interpreter*, by Amelia Defries (Routledge), 1927.

6

The seven phases were epitomized by the Greeks for both sexes, viz. :—

(E) Hebe	{ (the child	}	Eros (*M*) (Cupid)
Diana	{ the maiden boy	}	Hermes (Mercury)
Venus	{ the adolescent	}	Dionysius (Bacchus)
Minerva	maturity and wisdom		Apollo
Juno	{ with experience and in struggle for existence	}	Ares (Mars)
Ceres	{ fully skilled and with sorrows	}	Hephestos (Vulcan)
Sybil	{ senescent and with understanding	}	Zeus (Jupiter)

To each phase they built a temple, at the entrance to each of which it was possible to fall or stumble.

Christianity emphasized the fact that the passage from one temple to another is difficult, full of temptations and struggles, and thus enlarged the understanding of life.

Modern bio-psychology discerns that no life passes uniformly through all the phases. Most, indeed, cease development mentally at the third or fourth phase.

The life that has been sublimated in adolescence rises at maturity into a life of wisdom.

The genius is one who becomes indeed a God of Wisdom and engages, in the fifth phase, in a struggle for the existence of his ideas—on the battlefield of life.

In the sixth phase he is influencing and in the seventh phase seeing, the application of what, in the second phase, was a game, and in the third phase, a dream.

That, in a general way, is the course of passage, or pilgrimage, unconsciously followed by genius with its labour towards understanding—its clearing the way towards freedom of expression for the shedding of light upon truth. And in one form or another at each phase a sublimation takes place which can be compared to the taking of sacraments.[1]

* * * * * *

The course of life is direct—it is in action, rising through growth to maturity and thence sinking, throughout old age.

The curve of life is as definite as a mathematical figure—the main rise and fall are rhythmic and unavoidable, and so are its phases.

The periods of life vary a little, but are clearly marked by nature ; and no effort of man can substantially alter these.

The crises of life are four, and they come between the periods of life—and vary in each individual only by a few years one way or

[1] For details of this see *The Interpreter*.

8

another—and it is here that, in so far as we have any free will it is able to function.

The main forms of plant life are nine and are variously epitomized and accentuated in different plants, as :—swelling, shooting, leafing, branching, flowering, drying, &c., each arising at a crisis of life. The individual life-cycle contains for human beings, four social functions—PLAY ; QUEST ; MISSION ; PILGRIMAGE.

The first is common to us all : the second is of tremendous importance.

On the nature of the Quest in adolescence depends the life.

In a university in the colonies a student said to me once, with great excitement :—

" I'm going to get there ! "

" Get where ? " I naturally asked him.

" Get there. Get rich—make money ! "

So that was the nature of his Quest.

A pioneer is more likely to turn to the Quest of the Holy Grail in one form or another in youth. For even modern youth has in him " the need of a Wonder House,"[1] and, when above the ordinary, hitches his wagon to a star.

From the adolescent Quest (which to most of us ends with marriage) the clear development is towards a mission. The student may " get there " and get rich and get married—but he is not satisfied. He turns philanthropist,

[1] Haweis.

he collects art, he finances theatres or music, hospitals or politics—according to the dream of his youth ; but in all this he remains in the past. He is not a pioneer of science when he starts with such a Quest—unless he is a second Bacon. Genius entering in, transmutes the coin.

All of those pictured here developed a conscious Quest of their own, which logically worked out into a Mission and this Mission into a Pilgrimage—*along new paths of thought.* From the conception of the Quest to the last stages of the Pilgrimage, these men have hewn and laid the path over which they moved onwards towards freedom. Blazing their own trails, they are pioneers. Genius early develops a Quest : Genius always blazes a new trail. Fired by imagination it visualizes a new world and struggles to make it come true.

* * * * * *

Below the normal curve of life and its phases there may be the subnormal ; and there is the rare super-normal, which theology explains as the super-natural or convention leaves unexplained as " Genus," but which we are beginning to understand and, maybe, yet evoke.[1]

How far does genius follow one or all of these curves ?

[1] The above is my version of ideas I have gleaned from Geddes and from Branford, and which can be studied in detail at Le Play House, 65 Belgrave Road, S.W.1.

INTRODUCTION

In the human being there are ups and downs, scarcely accounted for by purely physical standards. Any life, however ordinary, may at one time or another balance perilously between the normal and the subnormal. Genius, with its tendency to soar above the norm to the super-normal, and with corresponding dangers of falls to below normal, is the most delicately balanced of all. And if, as the evolutionary biologist must claim, genius is the rise of the truly normal and all short of this is but sub-normal (roughly speaking) ; then the world produces very few normal beings ; and this norm, the genius, still stands in solitude, one amongst a million, by its nature without the support of the masses yet living for them.

If we study the contrast of the sexes we find essentially the same facts in the lives of both men and women, but each with a difference : and modern psychologists have seen that in every female there is more or less of the male and in every male something of the female. Character is partly determined by the degree in which one is present in the other.

And the degree changes in development of character, according as circumstances call forth the characteristic needed to meet the crisis and the phase : accident also may call out latent characteristics. And in a genius all this is infinitely more delicately adjusted, because less trammelled, than in ordinary mortals. Sometimes genius appears early. At other times it develops later.

In every life there are periods when the individual seems " finished " ; yet it is often in this dormant phase that inspiration comes. The bare trees in winter hold within themselves the hope of fresh growth, since above each leaf scar of last year we see the bud of spring. The spirit may be well nigh killed again and again while the individual lives. Sometimes it is killed beyond revival—as by some unconquered vice. Sometimes physical strength fails and with it mental power : sometimes conditions overpower it. Sometimes the spirit may but seem to die and lives again—as is proved in the life of every outstanding personality and even in the unknown lives of humbler people. Science cannot yet define the causes for all this and theology can at best only make inspired guesses. But the facts remain.

Inspiration is often the result of accident—like discovery. A chance word, a line read, a thing pursued for another purpose, inward accidents common to us all. Outward accidental happenings ; chance experiences ; unforeseen occurrences in the course of a moment of work . . . none of us escape these accidents. They are a law of life, common not only to human beings but to all that lives. Of the migratory birds how many fall by the way, the victims of circumstances ? Collision, as with a telegraph wire, may kill, or it may only maim ; the bird with a broken wing falls to the ground—sometimes to rise again and heal, marvellously. And during a lifetime what are the wounds inflicted on the wings of the soul ?

That soul, to the existence of which science has so little clue and about which religion and philosophy can only guess ! It is this that baffles psychology. Yet that there is in mankind this intangible " Something " who can disprove ?

The birds and the plants, like the animals, the metals, and the seas, are the victims of the elements. In the forest the very trees, in summer time, stand in constant danger of total suppression by fire—and this fear they share with many of the wild animals to whom they give their cathedral-like refuge.

To a very real extent, in modern times, man, by means of science, has gained control of the elements :—a steamship can run against the winds, the currents and the tides. We have won control—to a large degree—of fire. Water we turn to our own uses, almost at will. Air we can imprison and pump down to the diver many fathoms below the sea. By the discovery of how to use unseen waves in the ether we

can hear, see, and even move what is far
beyond our normal reach. This control of the
elements is one of the marvels of modern
science : yet even now the elements often
remain too much for man—causing famine,
pestilence and death which, so far, he is unable
completely to overcome.

Every individual is to a certain degree
subject to these elements. A sudden change
in the weather may destroy or kill a genius, as
it may finish off any man or animal or plant.
A social cataclysm, such as war, kills genius
and ordinary men alike : genius is far from
immune to disease. For the development of
character some of us need the pressure of
untoward circumstances to bring out latent
or inborn faculties. In some, as in certain
plants, the development is rapid ; in others
slow ; in some it is continuous ; in others
erratic.

The Elements, Circumstance, Accident, all
condition the behaviour and fate of man.
There are also the laws of heredity, only
beginning to be deeply considered. A simple
family will produce many children, of which
one only may be great. Genius, too, rarely
transmits genius. Hence to many it has seemed
that Nature uses up a superabundance of
energy in a genius ; for the children are seldom
other than ordinary mortals, despite the often

unusual environment in which they are reared.[1]

From this it looks, indeed, as though Environment had little to do with the formation of genius. The biology, not to say the eugenics of the problem, is still obscure. Genius usually conquers environment and seems in some cases to have conquered inherited weaknesses. Yet environment conditions the character of the genius—the circumstance of its historical period determines its nature : thus Lister and Pasteur arose when their cities (Edinburgh and Paris) were at their dirtiest.[2] Bacon arose amid confusion of thought. Leonardo thought and wrote when superstition was rife. Whenever and wherever the need is greatest, provision often seems made ; to the Hour, the Man. *Is this chance ?* Circumstance plays a large part in character —making or marring it.

> " *As iron sharpeneth iron*
> *So the friend shapeth the face of his friend.*"

Even the strongest characters are at some time in their lives moulded by their relatives and friends : even as they in turn mould

[1] Mrs. Soskice has pointed out to me that, owing to his absorption in his work and in himself, the children of a genius often have a sub-normal, even an unnaturally poor, commonplace environment.

[2] See *Cities in Evolution*, by Patrick Geddes (Williams and Norgate).

15

others with whom chance, or circumstance, throws them into contact. This is the Play of Life upon the individual, yet the gifted and strenuous individual also plays all the more on life. Inspiration often comes to irresolute spirits who cannot cope with the World : by it they and their inspiration are submerged. Genius is not always successful : it is contained in some of the saddest failures. It can be, and is, crushed. Genius is not unknown in lunatic asylums. Yet the saying that genius is akin to madness must not be taken literally ; most of us at one time or another in our lives tremble on the "Borderland"—our equilibrium is easily upset.

It is clear that in all potent characters there is a very definite and powerful sex-urge. In the full life-cycle of acts—facts—dreams and deeds,[1] a danger point often lies in the world of dreams.

From acts come experiences, and these when turned over in the mind develop ideas and thence again impulses and dreams.[2] Dreams often herald and call to action. Dreams demand outlet : if the outlet is not found they tend to run in a vicious circle and develop morbidly or run to seed. Here is the interior and most dangerous battlefield of life. The

[1] For full details of this see *The Interpreter*.
[2] This is developed from Prof. Geddes' well-known and suggestive theory set out in *The Charting of Life*.

outlet may be either upward or downward—
and at every crisis in life dreams may lead to
madness and hell ; or they may be transmuted,
by the process of sublimation (or in an older
word, " conversion "), to the highest deed, the
finest achievement ! The battle with Self is
surely harder, because stronger, in genius than
in simpler people ?

A career carried through to achievement is
nothing less than the Victory over Self, taught
by the prophets of old as the noblest conquest
possible to mankind. This conquest, then,
lies behind every victorious genius ; and is
at any rate in some degree a spiritual attain-
ment.

That is why, I think, we revere genius ; for,
whatever be the weaknesses of the individual,
to some extent the achievements of genius
have something of saint-like characteristics,
and embody the development of the spirit
despite failures and disillusion. Thus, in a
certain measure, modern scientists, and a very
few amongst artists, when pursuing the pure
search for truth, are the mystics of our day.

* * * * * *

Why do some men and women take the
hardest road, when gifted with faculties which
would ensure them success on easier lines ?
No study of genius can be complete without
an answer to this question.

Are they urged to self-sacrifice by personal ambition ? Is it because of the desire to be remarked as different from others ? Is it the Will to Power ?—which may not be mere ambition, but something finer—power over self, power over nature, which is even more satisfying, in the end, than mere power over money or over men. Is it the sporting spirit— the will to reach the goal unbeaten ? Is it love of excitement, pure and simple ? which in some people amounts to a ruling passion. (There can be few excitements to compare with that of the scientist on the verge of a discovery !)

Is it the will to Truth ? for which Buddha sacrificed not only himself and a kingdom—but his beloved wife.

Can all this be explained by the Freudian theory of dreams developed from sex-impulses alone ? Are the ductless glands enough to account for these manifestations of supreme selflessness ?

A genius, we must remember, often carves his way through uncongenial conditions—as of dull employment—to devote himself to what he feels to be his vocation ; sacrificing fortune or often even food—all comfort—even his feelings for his family, in so doing .In this he is like a monk who leaves the world for a life of prayer. This the rare scientist, and an isolated artist or so, does, that he may work at the thing he loves : his science is his happiness ; no relaxation, however necessary or welcome, can give him the same amount of pleasure.[1] He is like a boy engrossed in his favourite game ! In fact, his career is often the development of " a craze "—carried over from boyhood, started like a game. Started, then, in selfishness it develops into other worldliness.

Real happiness lies in increasing selflessness ; in the victory over Self—which is spiritual freedom. Is the sacrifice of the scientist, therefore, to be diagnosed as the search after such happiness ? Is the urge, when all is said, just instinctive, just Nature, which gives to rare specimens of the species, by pure chance, a different set of physical conditions ?

In that case, is Genius determined by what in ancient times was called Fate ?

But, remember, the instinct which produces genius can also, when inverted, produce great criminals, powerful leaders of vice.

If fate and chance account for everything, then there is, even in genius, no such thing as free will.

But if the element of choice comes in, if the moment comes when, caught in the vortex of dreams, a choice has to be made and a battle decisively won by one side or another, when

[1] For example : Faraday wrote of himself, " I, *for amusement*, learnt a little chemistry and other parts of philosophy, and felt an eager desire to proceed in that way further." (The italics are mine.—A.D.)

the urge has to be definitely sublimated if it is not to be inverted, then surely free will comes in ?

What conditions this momentous, irrevocable decision ? Science cannot explain.

A call is heard by the mind's ear ; a vision is seen by the mind's eye.

The classic explanation for this is summed up in old words :—it is the call of the supernatural—it is a vision sent by God.

And if genius is thus subject to, and the chosen instrument of, the supernatural, is it a matter of free will after all ?

These questions science cannot, so far, elucidate for us. They elude psychology and philosophy alike.

Genius, then, is subject to Heredity, yet to the Elements, to History throughout time, and to Environment of everyday Place, to Chance, and Accident, yet to Fate, and some tell us to the Supernatural, and thus, too largely as yet, seems a blind instrument in the hands of the unknown. It cannot be altogether accounted for by physical facts, nor yet by psychological or social theories.

Can modern psycho-analysis permanently maintain that all these diverse causes for the urge which drives a genius can be summed up and accounted for by the power of one set of organs in the body ? Can all its energies and will to power be explained as so many outcomes

INTRODUCTION

of the sex-instinct ? Must we not return to
that older and simpler view, as of the love of
the highest which we call God ? Bacon
certainly thought that some part of the sources
of our knowledge came through " Divine
Inspiration," and so far science has not been
able to find a better explanation. Even though
Voronoff says that loss of special glands causes
mental activities to deteriorate, this only
proves that the receptive faculties and physical
energies are fed by these glands : there is, so
far, no proof that these glands *create* the
inspirations of genius.

" *We are such stuff as dreams are made of,*"
but not even the Schools of Freud or of Jung
or others, have yet given us a conclusive
analysis of dreams—as the seven lives here
outlined go to prove.

Science can measure the energy of the atoms
in a star : but it cannot reach, much less
measure, the unknown cause of the energy by
which genius is driven !

AMELIA DEFRIES.

The Royal Institution of Great Britain,
21, Albemarle Street, W.1.
May, 1928.

"But there is a spirit in man; and the inspiration of the Almighty giveth them understanding."

Job xxxii., 8.

CHAPTER I

BOSE[1]

" The excessive specialisation of modern science in the West has led to the danger of losing sight of the fundamental fact that there can be but one truth, one science, which includes all branches of knowledge."

J. C. B.

INDIA holds the belief that whenever the country is in need the redeeming spirit will be reborn.

This belief has been a central idea in Indian thought for over four thousand years.

"Whenever the dharma decays and adharmna prevails, *then* I manifest myself . . . I am born again and again."

The rise and fall, the change, the decay and rebirth of enlightenment has always been understood in India. The peak is reached in one phase of civilization, gradually it decays,

[1] The study of electric waves ; anticipation of " Wireless " ; photography without light ; molecular change of matter under electrical stimulation ; universal sensitiveness inherent in matter ; unity of the organic and the inorganic ; the crescograph ; discovery of the nervous impulse in plants ; plant autographs and their revelations; on the irritability in plants ; the density of effects of drugs on plants and animals ; foundation of the Bose Institute.

23

and when it has sunken to its lowest level it
is re-infused with the old spirit renewed in new
terms and thus rises to a still higher peak.

India has always seen the vision of evolution,
of the progress possible to mankind. No matter
how far from all progress she has fallen at
various phases of her life, she has always kept
this central idea, this knowledge that the ashes
contain within themselves that deep-lying fire
which will again be blown into new life. India
has always known herself to be immortal.

The highest peak in her civilization was
reached thousands of years ago—when Europe
was mostly peopled by barbarians—in the
reign of King Asoka. Some at least tell us
that the lowest depth, if we count the condition of her masses, exists to-day. But the
spirit of the Asoka period is not dead. And
that is why there is more hope in India than
superficial or unfriendly observers, such as
Miss Mayo, would have us think.

Over and over again in history we have seen
a nation rise as one man, led by one man.
And even if to-day there existed among the
three or four hundred millions of Indians no
other leader, no other pioneer, than Sir Jagadis
Chunder Bose, there would yet be hope for
India.

On what do I base this statement ? On his
life, his work, his outlook, and on a few chance
words he once said to me : " I am trying," he

Library
I.U.P.
Indiana, Pa.

5oo.92 D362p
c. 1

BOSE

said quietly, " to turn out some men for the
service of the world—that's what I am for."
   Not for the service of science only, not for
the service of India purely—for the service of
the world. This impersonal attitude is entirely in keeping with the four thousand years
of Indian philosophy. It is easy to go the
round of hospitals and law-courts, even into
Parliament or business, or among the poverty-
stricken masses living with poor hygiene and
little food ; and it is easy to criticize the low
state of lip-service into which multitudes have
fallen in the carrying out of their religions.
We can admit, if we wish, the horrors depicted
in " Mother India," but that the philosophy is
not dead, that the spirit still liveth, is made
clear by the words of a man like this, standing
for what India is at heart. And there are
others, in other ways, bringing the dharmna
back again—for the sake of the whole world.
   Civilization first arose in India, and the
attitude to modern science of Sir Jagadis
Bose is a symbol of an attitude which is not
confined to him, and which will shed new light
over modern civilization.

   " Whenever the dharma decays . . .
   then I manifest myself "

And who is there shall say that in our Western
civilization, too, the dharmna is not decayed ?
The need is less obvious in the West, but that

it exists cannot be denied. Who shall say that the enlightenment which of old blew over the West from the East may not be about to proceed from the East again ?

All over the world to-day there are not wanting signs of a coming Rebirth, and the signs of the times may be read in India even more clearly than elsewhere, by those who have eyes to see.

Look back—for by the past we read the future.

There was a time, not so very long ago, when in Catholic Europe men might scarcely venture to believe that the earth moved, when such a man as Leonardo da Vinci was in danger of reprobation, when people were burnt at the stake, or put through the tortures of the Inquisition for daring to voice their independent ideas, and when Jews were subject to the last degrees of indignity and torture ; yet at that time in India even Atheism itself might be preached on the very steps of any Temple.

When in Catholic Europe any knowledge outside that of the established belief was so much feared, in India all knowledge was held to be a beatitude.[1]

But when modern science began, with its manifold wonders, and the manifold abuse of these wonders in application, India, lost in ancient memories, let it pass her by. It is a strange thing that the India where much of

[1] *The Web of Indian Life.*

26

science arose has not until now created a scientific movement.[1]

To understand a man, his work and character, and its significance, we must know something of the ancient tapestry of life from which he weaves his new pattern.

Why has an India, seeming so long deaf and blind to modern science, suddenly produced a man like Bose, more modern than our moderns, infusing science with a light it has, hitherto, scarcely known ?

Because there was a time when India was alive with similar men.

Patanjali, who wrote his great psychology in the second century, was obviously also a physiologist studying the living body in relation to that nervous system which, in its entirety of functioning, he would call the mind. His work was evidently the result of previous and more ancient investigations—a final record of long research.

The same is true of Indian mathematics—decimal notation is Indian in origin—and astronomy, surgery, and even chemistry, have notable records. The Law of Gravitation was enunciated by Acharya in the twelfth century ; since when apparently there have been no striking Indian discoveries till current time.[1]

But educated Indians know their classics, and behind the young Bose there stood a

[1] *The Web of Indian Life*, by Sister Nivedita (Longmans).

27

mighty web of intellectual tradition—original in its day, as epoch-making for ancient times as is our own newer scientific tradition to us, in the West, to-day.

So it happens quite logically that despite all there may be of a dying and chaotic India, as depicted by Kathleen Mayo, there comes a quiet vibrant figure, with the still small voice, a fighter too, who is a dreamer, an inventor more subtle in mind and hand than any Western man of science; and this is, naturally, the figure of a man who sees the world as One and who proclaims the unity of science.

And this impregnable figure not only shines like a lamp in his own country, but stands ahead of anyone in his own line of work throughout Europe and America. Sceptical at first—even prejudiced—and after denying him for twenty years, the Royal Society of London not only accepts his discoveries but crowns him with the most coveted of all scientific distinctions. He is almost the first Indian to be made a Fellow of the Royal Society. Westminster recognizes him, he is knighted by the King.

And in his own country an institute is set up according to his plans and rules; the Bose Institute in Calcutta stands to carry on what he initiates. He is a member of the Committee for Intellectual Co-operation of the League of

Nations. So, in Geneva, or in Paris, he and
Einstein meet—the one comparable to Harvey,
the other greater than Newton, and both products of our age ; and this is significant, that
the races to which these belong have produced
some of the great philosophies of all time ;
and on philosophy the fabric of civilization at
its best has been largely founded. Once a
year at least these two, whose towering minds
rise to the very stars, work together for the
peace of the world. And that this is so is,
strangely enough, a result of Armageddon.
" Patriotism is not enough "—for this the
millions died. Here East and West meet—
here civilization may be reborn.

Picture Bose, on his way to Geneva, with
new discoveries to tell to Einstein ; and
interested, too, in a whole world of university
development in Palestine to discuss with him,
wondering to himself whether, that year, the
Jew will be approachable. " His head will be
full of the Eclipse," the Indian said to me,
sighing. And picture Einstein, the Jew, on
his way from Berlin to the meeting, calculating
and calculating all the way, fearing that Bose,
the Indian, may not be interested in the
Eclipse—" His head may be too full of plants."

When two lions meet there is nothing left
but two tails !

That was the old way :—Pre-war. But
Geneva is established for peace—and even

29

lions carried beyond their personal interests may meet—because on new paths—in peace.

While Bose brings into Western science the intuitive vision of the East, Geddes takes to India the practical methods for the application of great ideas so typical of the West.

And in India Bose and Geddes meet. Two men, now, who see the unity of Science, the impossibility of separating mind from matter, who know, as the Hebrews of old declared— that Truth is one.

In the Arts, about this time, a similar meeting occurs in London : Tagore, who speaks neither French nor Russian ; Roerich, who speaks no English ; the one a writer, the other a painter, are able to understand each other (and they form an undying friendship), through the medium of the unity of their thoughts, expressed in their works. Behind the poverty of modern India, the chaos of modern Russia, the materialism of modern Europe, the intrigues of politicians and of financiers, the darkness of mass intelligence, the mammon-worship of America, all the time such meetings of the pioneers are going on—meetings which are laying the corner stones of a new enlightenment, of a world Renaissance !

And it is in America that a Roerich Museum is established ; so Mammon has his uses ; and, though finance very slowly turns toward the pioneers, the way of Rebirth is here being prepared. But these men will not touch commerce—they want nothing for themselves. Like the saints of old are these pioneers. By one of his first inventions Bose might have had a fortune. To-day he might be a multi-millionaire. But he chose otherwise. Offered a goodly sum if he would take out and sell a patent, he replied, " I would as soon sell my wife ! " He published his discovery like any other scientific paper—gave it for nothing for the service of the world. That is the honour of the profession of medicine since Hippocrates of old : it has no secret remedies, no patents.

Victor Branford wrote in his *Study of St. Columba*, " The Saints were poets *living* their poetry." And such a man is Jagadis Bose, for science may, and does at times, rise to the white heat of ecstasy of a kind unknown even to poets, but not unknown to saints. Untrammelled by the cold aloofness of Western scientific thought, the Indian is not afraid to raise the facts of life to the levels of poetry ; and whoever has read the Inaugural Address given by Bose when dedicating his Institute in Calcutta is aware that he stands in the presence of a very great poet indeed.

Poetry and religion are no longer divorced, but, as of old, are here made one. And so, in *The Voice of Life*, we have an old trilogy made new : Religion, Poetry and Science. And thus has Bose, without knowing it, worked out a portion of that " Charting of Life," which is Geddes' chief contribution to the *Unity of Thought*—and on which this trilogy appears as the chord of Inner life.[1]

And when he has filled himself with facts and proved his interpretations of them by experiment, in this world of the Cloister —the dream world—(which is the place of the Chord of the Inner Life), what does Bose do ?

Beyond this three-fold chord, on Geddes' chart, there is another—also three-fold, in the world of Deeds, for the chord of achievement is on the battlefield of life. Thus Bose comes out of his laboratory (his cloister), and, with the founding of his Institute, he expresses himself in Deed—in service to Humanity.

But this Institute needs the spirit, and the spirit needs its cloister ; and this Bose knows, alike by instinct and by experience. So while dedicating and organising his main centre in Calcutta, he keeps also his place for meditation high up in the mountains. Thus are the ideal and the practical made one.

And what a man can do a nation may do later.

" I dedicate to-day this Institute, not merely as a Laboratory but a Temple. . . . The

[1] See *The Interpreter : Geddes the man and his Gospel*, by Amelia Defries, p.   (Routledge, 1927).

32

little we can see is as nothing compared to the vastness of that which we cannot."[1]

Those are the opening words of his speech—on this note he sounds the chord for the music of Indian Science. And to his students he says :—
" There are truths which will remain beyond even the super-sensitive methods known to science. For these we require faith, tested not in a few years but by an entire life."[1]

He has established his Temple for the discovery of that truth for which faith is needed, in the belief that " when one dedicates himself wholly for a great object, the closed doors shall open, and the seemingly impossible will become possible for him."[1]

After thirty-two years of severe struggle, he voices this as his conviction :—
" It is not," he says, " for man to quarrel with circumstances, but bravely to accept them, and we belong to that race and dynasty who had accomplished great things with simple means."[1]

For twenty-three years he had kept the high resolve that " as far as the devotion and faith of one man counted, that would not be wanting," and so it came about that within six

[1] *The Voice of Life*, by Sir J. C. Bose, 1917.

33

months some of the most difficult problems connected with Electric Waves were solved in his laboratory. Those discoveries of Bose's were published by the Royal Society of London, and they, of their own accord, offered him an appropriation from their special Parliamentary Grant for the advancement of knowledge.

For five years after this, progress was uninterrupted—but then came a great change, for his investigations led him to the then amazing knowledge that the organic and the inorganic, the living and the non-living, always studied separately, with separate University Departments, were not really so separate! He discovered that " Inorganic matter was anything but inert." This seemingly simple discovery meant a revolution.

The gates opened to him by his first work now promptly closed against him. He had " unwittingly strayed into the domain of a new and unfamiliar caste system," and had offended its etiquette. He had discovered that " a universal reaction seemed to bring together metal, plant and animal under a common law."[1]

Filled with awe at this stupendous generalization he realized that he could prove scientifically that the world is one. That there is no fixed contrast of organic and inorganic—there is already in the apparently inert and in-

[1] *The Voice of Life.*

organic something of what we have always recognised as—*LIFE !*

With great hopes he went to announce this tremendous discovery to the Royal Society—demonstrated by experiments—but in course of so doing raised disapproval, and closed its doors against himself for twenty years ! It is fair to say he had met this criticism (very naturally) with a touch of sharpness, and so offended some of his seniors.

He was warned by physiologists to keep to the simpler domains of physics in which he had been winning approval rather than press his enquiries and results against their habitual preserves.

In a world blind to the triple chord of Religion, Science, Poetry, in a world where each one of these was established as an entirely separate thing, he was met by a very different chord—an unconscious theological, philosophical, and even scientific bias against him. A scientist not only stepping into the domain of a separate science, but even breaking the bounds long established by the philosophers, with their contrast of matter as " inert " and thus apart from life altogether.

To the popular theological bias against him was also added the distrust, and even fear, the British mind has about " the inherent bent of the Indian mind towards mysticism and unchecked imagination."

PIONEERS OF SCIENCE

Exactly the same blank wall which met Geddes' Charting of Life now met Bose's weaving of three parts of a third of this chart into a single science!

The average person, who does not yet realize into what watertight compartments each kind of knowledge has been packed by its experts, cannot conceive what such a discovery meant to some of these specialists. In England there are plenty of men of science with whom material things count for little—their difficulty was that their minds had grown into their pigeon-holes. Even a lion long in captivity cannot at first be made to credit, when placed in a larger cage, that he can pace further than the limits of his old one. Geddes has told me of seeing this at the Zoo he planned in Edinburgh, with one of the finest old lions who lowered his head and turned, as by habit he had always done, even though in the new cage there was no wall for him to come up against when he reached the end of his habitual stride. Thus some of the old lions of the Royal Society simply could not take in what Bose told them : they could not believe in the accuracy of his experiments nor realize the strength of his proofs. So at this period, outwardly, the career of Bose seemed " finished." At the height of his first success he had well nigh ruined himself. Yet he did not lose heart.

" It is forgotten," he wrote, " that He who

36

BOSE

surrounded us with this ever-evolving mystery
of creation, the ineffable wonder that lies
hidden in the microcosm of the dust particle,
enclosing within the intricacies of its atomic
form all the mystery of the cosmos, has also
implanted in us the desire to question and to
understand."[1]

And to the British misgivings about the mysticism and unchecked imagination of the
Indian mind, he replied, years afterwards,
" But in India this burning imagination which
can extort new order out of a mass of apparently contradictory facts, is also held in check
by the habit of meditation. It is this restraint
which confers the power to hold the mind in
the pursuit of truth, in infinite patience, to
wait, and reconsider, to experimentally test
and repeatedly verify."

In such writing he was dangerously en-
croaching on yet another tight-bound profession—for in those days was a scientist
expected to have such a gift for lucid, simple,
pure literature ?

One scientist here and there being mentally
vigorous among the hundreds of millions of
the Indian people, it may be said by Miss
Mayo's believers, is an exception, not a rule.
But even my small knowledge of Indians is
sufficient for me to know that Bose, though
outstanding by reason of exceptional genius,

[1] The Voice of Life.

37

is not an exception among the scientific, the
learned and thinking classes in India : where
he leads many are following.

The Indian mind is trained to withstand.
And Bose took his failure with inherited
philosophy and tolerance, saying : " It is but
natural that there should be prejudice, even in
science, against all innovations."[1]

He was prepared to wait till the wound
caused by the first shock of the blow had
healed—" till the first incredulity could be
overcome by further cumulative evidence."

Like a general who has lost a battle, he
withdrew his forces, retired and waited in
ambush, while new weapons were forged for
the next onslaught.

Retiring as he did to what is practically
another hemisphere, he was powerless, mean-
while, to remove the misrepresentations which
arose, and which followed him even to Calcutta.

For the next twelve years no conditions
could have been more hopeless than those
with which he was confronted. And in later
life he warns his students : " One who would
devote himself to the search for truth must
realize that for him there awaits no easy life,
but one of unending struggle."

What is it that causes men and women to
take up this life of struggle ?

What urge is there behind such a man as

[1] *The Voice of Life.*

38

Bose, and why is it that fresh students and searchers are never wholly wanting to take up their cross ?

Is it Ambition—to mark out a path and be different to others ? Would mere glory suffice for these characters ? Their history shows that is not what sends them forward.

Is it the will to Power ?

To attain power over nature is a grand thing ; to achieve power over self is even grander.

There is also undoubtedly much excitement in the quest : to be on the verge of a great discovery must be one of the most exciting adventures possible to mankind, and all these people work at a high pitch of cerebral excitement.

Psycho-analysis seeks to account for this by diagnosing it as a sex-impulse, of course highly sublimated. But sex-impulses, even when sublimated, do not usually work out in selflessness—neither does the love of power, neither does ambition.

The tremendous sacrifice demanded by the pure search for truth cannot be other than selfless.

What is it that produces this sacrifice of Self, seen again and again in the lives of modern scientists ?

It is not quite the same as the dangers and discomforts undertaken by those who fly, by those who go to the Poles. Explorers and flying men, people who, in danger of their lives, give up safety and comfort to break world records, or to discover new regions, these have a different psychology to those who patiently, if feverishly, work away in the solitude of their cloister or laboratory, and set their faces resolutely against publicity.[1] Those who take up pure research are in love with their science : theirs is clearly a labour of love.

Is it science for science's sake that explains their sacrifice of self ?

If so, then their labour is their pleasure, and may be explained as based on the Will to Pleasure—which is in all of us.

Is there more in it than this ?

Who shall explain the cause of the dreams of scientists, who are willing to give their lives to an Idea ?

Is it a purely impersonal love—the love of humanity—that makes a man or woman give away freely to the world what might be commercialized to bring the individual dis- coverer a fortune—which he disdains to take ?

Are those people physically, mentally, differently made from others ?

In a word, can modern psychology explain their urge by its too simple diagnoses and interpretations ?

[1] Bose never allows himself to be " interviewed ".

40

BOSE

Often a great discovery is in the first place an accident.

Bose was not seeking what he found. Madame Curie was not searching for Radium when she discovered it. Even the instruments for the experiments needed to prove such discoveries did not exist—had to be invented.

Years ago I remember hearing two famous scientists—Sir Edward Thorpe and Svante Arrhenius—talking about the discovery of Radium, and I think it was Thorpe who said, " It can only be put down to Divine Inspiration."[1]

Whence came the ideas which lead to such world-shaking discoveries ? Can they be explained as arising from the sex-impulse ? Or, are they not rather from another source, a source which science does not handle or try to explain—namely, the Supernatural ? Has not the Roman Catholic Church the secret, both of diagnosis and of discipline of these types, in its age-long and well-planned system of the Vocations ?

The love of spiritual research, then, would appear to arise from the least understood branch of psychology — one which science has not elucidated — namely, the supernatural. And scientists who devote themselves to the search for even a particle of truth, do so because they cannot help it, because they are but the instruments of an

[1] As Sir Francis Bacon thought.

Inspiration, urging them to this Vocation—
that they may work out a call from a region
for the existence of which they can offer no
explanation.

If this is so, then are they not the mystics
of the modern world ?

When one sees the face of a man like Bose,
as he gives his lectures, transformed like that
of a poet, lit up with what can only be described
as the love of God, while he explains his experiments—when one reads the words in which
he dedicates his Temple, it seems as though
this explanation, unscientific though it may
be, is the true one. Such men are the priests
of modern life—the Teachers of the modern
world, following an inborn instinct which
cannot be physically explained—the servants
of a Supernatural Intuition.[1]

Thus the newest science and the oldest
religion come very near together at last. Both
are moved by the same urge ; both have,
fundamentally, the same faith, though in
doctrine they may differ.

Speaking of the type he represents, Bose
says : " It is for him to cast his life as an
offering, regarding gain and loss, success and
failure, as one ".[2]

---

[1] As Faraday said—but regarding the " supernatural," I
get a newer view from Geddes, who sees it as " all quite
natural " and who divides the natural into two :—(a) " Supreme " and (b) " Fundamental " ; (a) " The Mystical, or old
Supernatural " ; (b) " The Organic, or the old Natural ".
[2] *The Voice of Life.*

In India (alike for Indians and their rulers, too), barren of science and poor in the necessary instruments and conditions for carrying on new scientific work, the difficulties with which Bose was now faced were heavy indeed, bitter and well nigh crushing. But those very difficulties only strengthened his determination to succeed, and to make less arduous the path of those who should follow him ; in this high resolve he was moved by a nobler urge—the urge of a soldier in war.

" That India is never to relinquish what has been won for her after years of struggle ".

To the passion for truth, in his case, was added the passionate love of country. In his " dedication " he points out that success and power, in the vortex of international competition, vital though this is (for he recognizes that neglect of industrial enterprise may imperil her very existence), will not alone insure the life of a nation. He criticizes the feverish rush of the West for " exploiting applications of knowledge not so often for saving as for destruction ", passionately declaring that " in the absence of some power of restraint civilization is trembling on the brink of ruin ".

Here for a moment the scientist turns politician—but towards the Etho-Polity of Geddes' dream—in this helped by an ancient national philosophy. Here East and West meet and understand each other—together they sow the seeds of the coming World-Polity.

Listen to Bose once more, as in his high, small, quiet voice with clear diction he develops this theme, like a High Priest :

" (Man) has followed the lure and excitement of some insatiable ambition . . . he forgot that more potent than competition was mutual help and co-operation in the scheme of life ; and in this country (India) through millenniums there have always been some who, beyond the immediate and absorbing prize of the hour, sought for the realization of the highest ideal in life—not through passive renunciation, but through active struggle . . . He alone who has struggled and won can enrich the world by giving away the fruits of his victorious experience ".

Is this a scientist speaking ? Or is it an inspired teacher of Religion ? May not the two be one ?

" This I know," he goes on, " that no vision of truth can come except in the absence of all sources of distraction, and when the mind has reached a point of rest."

Was it not in this very spirit that the Monastic Orders were founded by the Saints centuries before ?

Here indeed we have the spirit renewing

44

itself—" *Whenever the dharma decays . . . then I manifest myself, I am born again and again !* "

" For my disciples," the scientist[1] says, " I call on those very few, who, realizing some inner call, will devote their whole life with strengthened character and determined purpose to take part in that infinite struggle to win knowledge for its own sake and see truth face to face—with the ideal of giving, enriching; in fine, of self - renunciation, in response to the highest call of humanity."

Is it not thus that the Buddha might speak if suddenly reborn into this modern scientific world ?

THE WORK

In the work already carried out in Bose's laboratory the wonders of the highest animal life have been fore-shadowed, in the response of matter and th *unexpected* revelations in plant life ; and very extended regions of enquiry in Physics, in Physiology, in Medicine, in Agriculture, and even in Psychology, have been opened out. Problems hitherto regarded as insoluble have been brought within the sphere of experimental investigation by his dual point of view, his alternating, yet

[1] Sir J. C. Bose.

45

rhythmically unified interaction of biological thought with physical studies and of physical studies with biological thought.[1] The whole scope of organic and inorganic science has been enlarged and opened out by Bose's understanding of their unity. " High success," he tells his disciples, " is not obtained without corresponding experimental exactitude ".[1]

This is perhaps the fundamental difference between modern and ancient thought.[2]

No matter what may be the dream, the inspiration, the vision, or the flight of imagination, the capacity for receiving revelation, of a modern scientist (even a mystical Indian dreamer) he cannot accept any truth unless he is able to prove it exactly and beyond a doubt, not by reasoning or by argument, but by physical and accurate demonstration. He has to capture the spirit and make it man. An inspired guess in the dark must be turned into exact knowledge and find its verification in life.

It was not enough for Columbus to be convinced that his way across the world existed— he had to find it and prove its existence, not

[1] *The Voice of Life.*
[2] " The greatest care must be taken that the mind be absolutely free from preconceived ideas. Nature is only to be conquered by obedience—man must be merely responsive. God forbid that we should give out a dream of our own imagination for a pattern of the world."—Sir Francis Bacon.

BOSE

merely to the mind's eye, but to the eye of the body.

And this is what every scientist has to do with his reasoned theories or vivid guesses.

And Bose, when he had made his first unexpected discovery, was forced to invent new instruments by which he could prove to the eye what his mind had perceived. And he has therefore designed a long succession of super-sensitive instruments and new combinations of apparatus, which now tell of the protracted struggle " to get behind the deceptive seeming into the reality that remained unseen ".[1]

Picture to yourself the continuous toil and persistence and ingenuity of the scientist, forced by circumstances to become inventor, in his fight to overcome his human limitations!

In the more than a hundred and fifty different lines of investigation carried on by Bose during twenty-three years, it was only after nearly a quarter of a century's work that he fully realized that in them there was a natural sequence! " The study of Electric Waves led," he tells us,[2] " to the devising of methods for the production of the shortest electric waves known. These bridged over the gulf between visible and invisible light ; from this

[1] *The Voice of Life.*
[2] *The Voice of Life.*

47

followed accurate investigation on optical properties of invisible waves ; and his invention of a new type of self-recovering electric receiver was the forerunner of the application of crystal detectors for extending the range of wireless signals.

In physical chemistry he detected a molecular change in matter under electrical stimulation and this led to a new theory of photographic action. And the " fatigue " of his receivers led him to the discovery of the universal sensitiveness inherent in matter, as shown by its electrical response.

After this he was able to study this response, under changing environment, " its exaltation under stimulants and its abolition under poisons are among the most astounding outward manifestations ".[1]

Like a child listening to a fairy tale is the scientist before the wonder of the facts revealed to him as the result of his impersonal experiments !

Metals get tired, they feel, they can be made drunk, they can be poisoned. Is inorganic matter dead ? For the first time it was possible to prove the contrary !

This discovery has had many valuable applications, useful to mankind and also to commerce.

A single example may be given.

[1] *The Voice of Life.*

BOSE

" The characteristics of an artificial retina "
(which he had made) " gave a clue to the unexpected discovery of ' binocular alteration
of vision ' in man : each eye thus supple-
ments its fellow by turns, instead of acting
as a continuously yoked pair, as hitherto
believed."[1]   And so the work-in-evolution
developed.

The next step was a long study of the activities of plant-life as compared with the corresponding functioning of animal life—and the
very close and hitherto undreamt of unity
between man and the plants by whose life he
lives, was revealed.

Plants which for the most part seem motion-
less or passive are, in truth, not so !

To prove this he invented a special apparatus of extreme delicacy, to magnify the tremor
of excitation and also to measure the per-
ception-period of a plant to the thousandth
part of a second.

This instrument is one of the most delicate
ever made and possibly only the subtlety
of an Indian mind could ever have conceived
it, and made it work.

So Bose began his measurements and records
of ultra-microscopic movement, the length
measured being often smaller than a single
wave-length of light; and at length he
achieved the astounding feat of making the

[1] *The Voice of Life.*

49

plant fully write the record of its own sensations ![1]

" The secret of plant life was thus for the first time revealed by the autographs of the plant itself ", he tells his students as modestly as if he had had nothing whatever to do with it.[1]

To use his own words, this evidence of the plant's own script removed the long standing error which divided the vegetable world as supposed insensitive from the animal world as sensitive.

His investigations showed that all plants, even trees, are fully alive to changes of environment and respond definitely and speedily to its stimuli. They are aware even of a passing cloud—indeed in this they are far more sensitive than human beings !

In short, in this series of discoveries, Bose has completely established the fundamental identity of life-reactions in plant and animal. This is seen in a similar periodic insensibility in both, corresponding to what we call sleep, as seen in the death-spasm, which takes place in the plant as in the animal ; and this unity is further seen in the spontaneous pulsation of plant-cells, which in the animal combines and develops to the heart-beat ; it is seen in the identical effects of stimulants and of

[1] See *Plant Autographs and their Revelations*, by Sir J. C. Bose (Longmans, 1927).

anæsthetics ; and of poisons in vegetable and
animal tissues.

American papers have headlined Bose as the
man who can make a carrot drunk : but the
results of his discoveries are far more important
than that, and will slowly revolutionize agriculture and horticulture. Thus, for vivid
example, it has so far been almost impossible
to transplant old trees ; but Bose gives them
an anæsthetic much as a surgeon gives his
patients chloroform. He can then remove
them, operate on them, and replant them without shock to them, and consequently without
killing them. Such trees are now growing
as well as ever in the garden of his Institute.

" This physiological identity in the effect
of drugs is regarded by leading physicians
as of great significance in the scientific advance
of Medicine : since here we have means of
testing the effect of drugs under conditions
far simpler than those presented by the patient,
far subtler too, as well as more humane than
those of experiments on animals."

In short, he has paved the way to the abolition of vivisection of animals by substituting
a fresh method of gentler experiment, upon
plants.

One of the instruments he invented towards
achieving all this is called the Crescograph ;
and by this refinement of the old ways of
growth-measurement, sometimes up to a

millionfold, he sees how to advance practical agriculture, since for the first time it makes possible the separate study of the many conditions which modify the rate of plant growth. Experiments which formerly needed seasons or months, and then with their results vitiated by unknown circumstances and changes, can now be carried out in a few minutes. The dreamer, the experimenter, thus appears as more practical than the " practical man ". Kipling is right :—

> " *Drawbridge let fall!*
> *He's the lord of us all*
> *The Dreamer whose dreams come true* ".

And now a new and unexpected chapter of his life-work is opening out from the demonstration he has made of the nervous impulse in plants. He has determined its speed, and has measured the plant's nervous excitability and the variation of that excitability, exactly. The nervous impulses in plant and in man are exalted or inhibited under essentially similar conditions.

He finds, too, that a plant carefully protected under glass from outside shocks, though it looks sleek and flourishing, is really weakened, if not almost *effete !* But when a series of blows is rained on this pampered specimen, the shocks themselves arouse anew the deteriorated nature : " And is it not," he asks,

" shocks of adversity, and not cotton-wool protection, that evolve true manhood ? " Here then, we may learn how to treat our own nervous system by studying that of the plants.

Still he goes on experimenting ; and next he comes to a great mystery which has long puzzled physiologists and psychologists alike —the mystery which underlies Memory. For by his experiments it is now possible to trace " memory impressions " backwards *even* in inorganic matter, and to prove such latent impressions to be capable of subsequent revival.

Investigation on the nervous impulse in plants has led to the discovery of a controlling method, which was found equally effective in regard to the nervous impulse in animals.

Thus he has proved that the lines of physics, of physiology, and of psychology converge and meet—and has demonstrated unity in variety. And he thinks that " here it is the genius of India should find its true blossoming ", proving by modern science that in all its diversity nature is One.

And thus, from a demonstration of discoveries so marvellous as to be at first literally incredible to most of our Western men of science, he advances from exact science, more *minutely* exact than science had ever been before, quite naturally into the realm of

PIONEERS OF SCIENCE

pure philosophy; saying, finally, like a prophet, as a conviction based on experiment :

" The past shall be reborn in a yet nobler future ".

And he stands as a symbol of modern Indian science making possible the vision of ancient Indian thought :

" I am born again and again ".

THE MEANS

Jagadis Bose, like many another man of science, does not want money for himself—but money for his work is a necessity. Science is not a luxury and its cost is small, even infinitesimal when counted beside what the world gains in actual wealth, let alone health, by its development.

While conducting these extraordinary investigations he had at the same time to consider his financial problems, at times almost overwhelming, and to find the finance needed to carry on the work, without lowering his standard, without deviating from his ethical position.

When at the outset his success in the realm of the physicists won him the praise of Lord Kelvin, Lord Rayleigh and other leaders in that profession, the Royal Society placed a

54

grant at his disposal, and published his discoveries. But when by removing the barri-
cades between physics, physiology, and even
psychology, he only succeeded in puzzling
the magnates of the Royal Society, the support
they had given him was no longer forthcoming.
So many different branches of science did not
wish to be made one ! He could not go back
on what had been revealed to him. He was
almost in the position of Galileo—for though
scientists are not imprisoned in modern times
when their discoveries upset tradition, they
can be " sent to Coventry ".

After a long period of struggle, the gloom
was suddenly lifted by his being sent on a
scientific deputation, in 1914, from the Government of India. This provided the opportunity for him to give experimental demon-
strations of his discoveries before the leading
scientific societies of the world. These led to
the acceptance of his theories and results ;
and it is characteristic that when describing
this, he says : " This led to the recognition of
the importance of the Indian contribution
to the advancement of the world's science."

India's four hundred million people are thus
broadly represented to the West, so far as its
best thought and science are concerned,
by one unbending man ; and he at once
subordinates and realizes himself in spiritual
union with India—past as well as present.

55

And because India has had so great a past
it is impossible for him to do otherwise !

" I came with nothing and with nothing I
shall return," Bose says : and that line might
well be a passage from the Vedas.

He has given all he had of family fortune
and of earnings alike ; and his noble and beautiful wife, who has shared with him all his
struggles and all his hardships, has similarly
devoted all that is hers for the same object.
Thus in his struggling efforts he has never
been entirely solitary. While the world
doubted there have been a few who never
wavered in their trust ; and of these few the
first was Lady Bose.

Does Miss Mayo tell of one such ideal
Indian marriage of twin souls ?   And where
there is one there must be many more. This
alone shows how false and misleading are her
pictures of Indian life. It may be that such
perfect unions even in India, are the exception—as too much in all countries—yet
exceptional people are the leaders of every
nation.

In answer to the need of material support
for the Research Institute, response came at
last. The Indian Government awoke to
sanction grants towards placing the Bose
Institute on a permanent basis ; and the
extent of its grants will be proportionate to
the public interest taken in what is now a

general Indian undertaking. People to whom
he is personally unknown—princes and mer-
chant princes among them—sent donations ;
and the general feeling which his work is beginning to arouse is shown by a little contribution
from two girl students in a Western Province
of India, sent to him " for the service of our
common motherland ". Even a solitary way-
farer in the Himalayas remembered to send
him a message. And yet now he does not
know—except by feeling—what it is that has
"bridged over the distance and blotted out all
differences ".

It was in 1901 that the news went out to
India from London—in crude and exagger-
ated form—" Bose's work and paper are re-
jected by the Royal Society ", " and thus," says
his biographer, " of course, suspicion was
thrown on his previous work as well."[1]

Gradually he was recognized by his Europ-
ean peers, but it has taken almost twenty years
for the truth of his work to make its way
completely into the light.

When at length he was recognized over
Europe as well as throughout the British
Universities, suddenly and with almost drama-
tic unanimity and completeness, the Royal
Society appreciated the man for whom nearly
a quarter of a century it had delayed to recog-

[1] *The Life and Work of Sir Jagadis C. Bose*, by Patrick
Geddes (Longmans).

E

nize! In 1920 Bose was elected a Fellow of the Royal Society. Victory—at last!

To him not a mere personal battle, but victory for India. Yet, the urge which led him all the time was more than mere patriotism —it was inspired and fed by a living faith—a faith, in ideas and ideals, four thousand years old, in him renewed and living still.

Imagine him at the outset—in a country where science as a career was still rarely heard of (he who as a child had often been too fascinated by some outdoor nature-interest and beauty to come in to his food) after some years teaching in the Presidency College at Calcutta, on his thirty-first birthday fully resolved that his life henceforth was to be above all dedicated to the pursuit of new knowledge.

He could get no proper laboratory and the only available assistant was an untrained tinsmith! Yet within three months he had devised and constructed original apparatus for his first research. It was in recognition of the value of these researches that the University of London conferred on him its Doctorate of Science without examination.

And it was at this time that his vision of establishing an Institute of Science in India came to him. To others this appeared a mere dream and so, once more, he and his devoted wife agreed to continue their mutual life of

privation and sacrifice so that he might—at
some future time—be able to set going a
modern revival of India's ancient scientific
tradition.

He was still an education officer—his research work had to be done after a long day's
teaching. No grant was available. From
his own slender income he had to find money
for the making of his apparatus and for paying
his assistants.

Such work never goes quite unnoticed, and
the attention of the Lieutenant-Governor of
Bengal was attracted. Prejudice was strong
against Bose. The Governor's first proposal
was cancelled. But in the end he succeeded in
getting the Government to do something. It
offered to pay the expenses of research which
had redounded to its credit.

But it was dealing with a man of spirit!
Bose gratefully declined to accept any re-
muneration for his past work. Then the
Government sanctioned an annual grant (£166)
towards the expenses of his future research,
which was accepted.

It was the same Lieutenant-Governor who
at length, and after overcoming difficulties,
sent him for a much-needed change, in the
guise of a scientific deputation to Europe, for
six months.

It was the first time that the Government of
India had done anything for Indian science.

59

All these difficulties came from without. But what of the difficulties from within ? Who but a scientist can even begin to imagine the extreme trial of strength, as it were, this pioneer had set himself in the struggle with his own science or the extraordinary difficulty of the investigations he evolved for himself ?

Investigations which in application have immense bearing upon the future of the world, and in all manner of ways, even " practical ", as from advancing industries to increasing food supplies.

One example only : the study of the movement of growth in plants. On an average it takes a thousand years for a tree's growth to cover a mile. The slowness of a snail is proverbial, but its pace is 2,000 times faster than the average movement of growth—in a word, the plant grows at the rate of half the length of a single wave of light.

How devise an instrument to measure anything so slight ?

The instrument still used in the botanical laboratories of the West would magnify about twenty times or so. No use to Bose.

After eight years of labour he perfected his High Magnification Crescograph, devised a new form of necessary suspension for it, and was then able to magnify 10,000 times !

BOSE

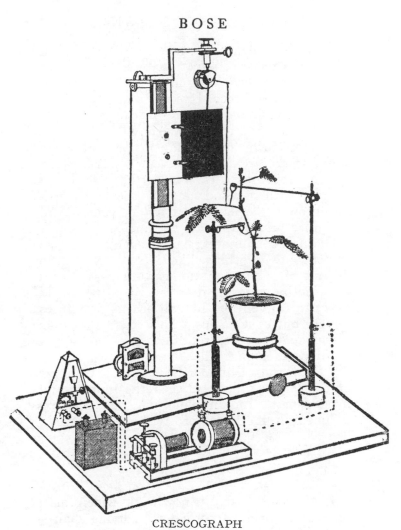

CRESCOGRAPH

From *Life and Work of Sir J. C. Bose,* by Patrick Geddes,
(by permission of Messrs. Longmans, Green and Co., Ltd.).

61

This instrument attached to a plant, with pencil and piece of paper enables the plant to make its own growth chart. By this means, too, it can itself record its reaction to environment, alcohol and poison—it can record its excitement—and its death agony !

The invention of such an instrument alone is one of the greatest achievements ever made by any inventor. It was further developed by him until it could magnify the imperceptible growth of plants ten million times, and has since been improved yet farther.

Our mind cannot grasp a magnification so stupendous. Nothing like it had ever been dreamt of. It meant unheard-of possibilities to scientific investigation all over the world —yet this invention, like all others, he refuses to sell, but says to his fellow scientists—take it—make it—use it, free of charge.

No wonder that the *Times* wrote :

" Sir Jagadis Chunder Bose is a fine example of the fertile union between the immemorial mysticism of Indian philosophy and the experimental methods of Western Science ".

The Man

In the face of what is now world-wide praise, of a kind rarely accorded to a living man— and never before given to a man of science

from India—Bose, grizzled, worn, not always
in good health, but with still shining eyes,
with a face often lit up by the glow of the love
and faith which have moulded his life, remains
impersonal.

The fruits of his own success pass over his
head—his mind's eye is fixed on the future.
He alone sees the great vision of what he cannot
live to complete :

" The outlook is endless, for the goal is at
infinity. The realization cannot be through
one life, or one fortune, but through co-operation of many lives and many fortunes."

His face has in it all sadness, all pity ; and
tolerant understanding. The victor in such
valiant battles—there is nothing of triumph,
nor of bitterness in him. He is not exactly
fine-looking—but his expression exhales a
spirit of sheer beauty when he talks—when
for instance he shows you that celery is easily
tired ; when he puts before you the autograph
of a growing dahlia ; or proves to you that
the rise of the sap in every plant has a pulsation which recalls the heart of an animal[1]—or,
if you like, how he discovered that metals may
suffer from fatigue. The whole wonderful set
of life-revelations for which he is responsible
appears to be to him like a poem someone else
has written, yet which has touched him very
deeply.

[1] *Plant Autographs and their Revelations*, by Sir Jagadis
Bose (Longmans).

He seems at times almost imperceptible himself, so lost is he in his subject, as when he tells of the response of plants to wireless stimulation ! (What a subject for great poetry is untouched here !) Imagine this solitary, intangible, impregnable Indian at work in his early days, at the invitation of Sir J. Dewar and Lord Raleigh, in Faraday's Laboratory at the Royal Institution. The first Indian scientist ever accepted by Western men of science as their equal. The immense history behind him, the dim prestige around him— himself impervious and non-attached. And then his upsetting of various professional applecarts—and retiring to India for twenty years, working all alone. For there was not then in his University or indeed in all India a single colleague to work with him. The man who anticipated " Wireless," and who suceeded (in 1901) in taking photographs without light— had not a soul in his country with whom he could discuss his ideas and experiments. Is it of him or of some other scientific giant the story is told that, asked how many people could understand his work, the answer came :

"In all the world I only know of one man who can understand me—and he misunderstands me."

It seems that not a man, but a mountain only, could stand the strain of such isolation ; but by his side there was one who has stood by

BOSE

him in all his struggles—his wife, who in her immovable serenity, in her beautiful antique costume of bronze and gold, is like some old Indian painting come to life; gentle, yet like a queen in her quiet smiling dignity. She too has sacrificed herself for the advancement of human knowledge, and thus found further happiness.

"Never can you find truth," said Bose to me, " until your mind, after long discipline, is dropped to a state of lethargy—and," he added, " never be diverted by personal ambition. You have to be a mere witness, you are the witness of truth—and this requires a long time, until you can wipe out all the littlenesses which distract your progress. This big idea of getting free is twenty-five centuries old," he ended softly.

Such is the man whose one rule for the workers in his Temple is that no patent shall be taken out ; and that all inventions must be made public ; whose students must offer their lives' services to humanity, as soldiers on the battlefield, in the great fight against Ignorance.

" It is not true," he told me another time, " that science wipes from the face of Natire the veil of awe. We are not tearing down the great mystery—we are but trying, little by little, to elucidate this mystery. But," he said carefully, "we must not go in for mere mysticism— we must be exact."

One day, after a lecture, annoyed by some stupid people who could not respond to his explanations, he said of them, " Yet radishes vigorously answer ! They are like chloro-formed radishes—if you can imagine any animal as stupid as a radish ! " And a quick smile, like that on the face of a boy, lit up his lined face. " You see," as if to explain away his temporary irritation, " plants are ten times more sensitive than human beings. I think, however, though they can see more than we can, that plants are deaf."

When his sense of humour has free play it is easy to find in him still something of the frivo-lous youth at Cambridge, who was always absent-minded ! And then, he will be quickly serious again : " I must forget what I have done—to get new vision—in Art it's the same thing."

This is the man whose little experimental garden at his country cottage down the Ganges from Calcutta is pointed out by the villagers : " There—in there—that is where the plants talk to him."[1]

This is the man who, in 1895, anticipating " Wireless," in a public lecture in Calcutta, demonstrated the ability of electric rays to travel round the lecture room through the body of the chairman and three solid walls, leaving

[1] *The Life and Work of Sir Jagadis C. Bose,* by Patrick Geddes (Longmans, Green and Co.).

BOSE

the receiver energy enough, at this distance, to set a bell ringing, discharge a pistol, and explode a miniature mine . . . AND TOOK OUT NO PATENT!

But the plants claimed him; and it was through them that he was able to rediscover—and to prove exactly—the Unity of Life.

The Pioneer is as dust before the magnitude of the revelation.

CHAPTER II

GEDDES

" There is no cure-all, no patent remedy ".
P. G

AN agile, thin young man (seventy-three years
of age), swift in movement and sudden in action,
with gentle, sad, tired eyes glowing beneath
shaggy eyebrows, wiry hair on end, pulling at
his shaggy beard with tireless hands, paces in
his garden on the summit of a hill outside
Montpellier and surveys the wide horizon
while considering the immediate problem of
the moment, and at the same moment attend-
ing to the planting which is his life's recreation.
He is a prophet in exile. And, as he surveys,
he talks. He talks ceaselessly, sometimes so
gently that his words are lost in his beard,
sometimes so fiercely that, as his pacing suddenly comes to a stop and he confronts his
listener, trembling with righteous rage, his
eyes literally blaze with passion.[1]

Can this ready, scintillating wit, this eager
blaze of energy, this white heat of creative

---

[1] This same excitement, rapidity and precision of conversation, was seen in Sir Humphrey Davy.

68

power, really come from a man of over
seventy ?

His children, fearful for him, have urged him
to retire.

" Daddy, you have fought long enough,"
they have said. " Come home to us on your
Castle-hill at Edinburgh, and let us take care
of you, and give you rest."

" I am still on the battlefield of life," is the
reply, almost hissed out from between obstin-
ately closed lips—he has the mouth of a satyr !

In his youth he had dreamed a dream, seen
a vision, so vast that while there is life in him
he must battle on, always hoping to make this
dream come true.

> " I will not cease from mental fight,
>   Nor shall my sword sleep in my hand,
> Till we have built Jerusalem
>   In England's green and pleasant land ".

Blake's verses might be emblazoned on the
shield of Geddes—with this difference, his
vision encompasses the entire universe ! Here
we have a professor who " specialises in
omniscience."[1]

All over the world, to-day, people are asking
" Who is Patrick Geddes, what does he stand
for ? " Yet he remains the most unknown—
obscure even to the mass—of all pioneers and
students.

[1] The late Israel Zangwill—see Preface to *The Interpreter*.

Why is this ?

Because he has always run away from publicity, and when, at rare intervals, it has been forced upon him, he has complained of being skinned alive ! His real interest, like the children's, is in the next game, not in the last one ; and so, too, it is the new research rather than the finished and published one, that matters to him. It is like the artist's enthusiasm for the next picture ; and research cannot be made public, in his view, until it has proved workable, and been applied ; by which time he frees himself of it, and is on the track of something else.

He pleads : " . . . And so, above all, peace and quietness for this. That is the very meaning of the cell, the hermitage, the cloister, the study, the laboratory, through the ages. You Londoners talk endlessly of Politics and Capital and Labour—but what makes your Parliament so futile (to-day most of all) and Capital and Labour alike too sterile (save of money quarrels), is just that they have no study to retreat into, and thus no fresh thought to offer. But in Science—perhaps most of all just now for social solutions—we need in the most real sense to revive the monastic discipline for ourselves and not simply its hospitality for others. Press methods not only killed poor Langley with its sneers at his aeroplane, it does worse : it has spoiled Edison, largely ;

GEDDES

and Burbank almost altogether—and so it is
spoiling the younger generation too : so leave
me at peace in my cloister to think out and
prepare the better city, the renewing university ! . . ."[1]

But now after more than half a century of
ceaseless battling with himself in his cloister,
and on the field of life, too, people all over the
world are beginning to ask about him, to want
to see this very tangible force behind so many
steps in modern progress.

From all over the earth, from India and
Dundee, Paris and Mexico, New York, Jerusalem, Johannesburg, Montreal, London, Mel-
bourne, Manchester, Berlin and Rome, there
come, at intervals, the written opinions of
authorities in various branches of arts and
sciences, comparing Patrick Geddes to Darwin,
Galton, Newton, Leibnitz, Pythagoras, Aristotle, Socrates, Sir Francis Bacon, and even to
Leonardo da Vinci.

Each specialist sees him mirrored in his own
particular speciality—for he encompasses them
all ! " But," says a London writer, " there
is one word which sums him up—perhaps
the most defiled word in the world—politics."[2]

His hatred of publicity is not the only reason
for his seeming obscurity. We have seen how

[1] *The Interpreter.*
[2] *The Daily News.*

71

Bose had to wait twenty years for recognition because he saw the inorganic and the organic sciences as indivisible, proclaimed the Unity of Science, and brought Religion to this wedding.

What, then, can we expect for Geddes—one of the fathers of modern geography, and of much in modern psychology and biology, who sees no dividing line between Politics, Ethics, and Education ; no separating barrier between Religion, Sciences and Arts, or between Labour and Capital, save arranging them all as developing in and from the common world of Folk—Work—Place ; who in his " Charting of Life," proves that there are no separate individual-isms possible, no separation between the classes and the people—no walls to separate Science from Art, Labour from Intellect, or those from the inner life ; and thus no sterilizing of the spiritual forces which arise from these, to remould the world and its governments upon the plane of Deeds and Achievements.

Of course, the learned Societies do not yet ask him in !

" Geddes is a figure apart in modern science . . . his vision is penetrating many minds . . . It is unfortunate that the scientific world can bestow no honour that would quite fit the case of Geddes, though its debt to him is seen in the manifold utilisation and development of his thought, not seldom used by workers who scarcely know his name ".[1]

[1] *Nature.*

GEDDES

No Fellowship of the Royal Society for this man, to include whose interests and activities each distinct card index and catalogue would be needed, and a new one made!

Card indexes, whether in publishers' or in Government offices, cost money to make, and once made are not lightly thrown over : the machinery of organization by which the present-day world is run is a very costly thing, and cannot be thrown away or remade in a day.

There is no room in the world as it is for he who "specializes in omniscience," and some would say that to make room would mean no less than force—if not even revolution.

Geddes is no believer in Revolution. As a student of nature and an evolutionist of the first order, he knows that vital changes, to be profitable, come slowly, and in the order of natural growth. He often tries to set the young revolutionist to watch a bulb growing or to observe the buds in spring.

To give him an exact label, he is a biologist— " an obscure professor of botany "—but " he ranges outside the strict limits of his science into the fields of practical sociology, into statistics and economics, the dramatization of history, peace and war, civics and architecture, psychology and ethics, politics, the vexed coal crisis, and most of all with town-planning ;

and who shall say that these divergences are outside the field of biology ? "[1]

" One might get the impression," writes an American, " that Professor Geddes is a vigorous institution, rather than a man."[2]

He is difficult to follow, because he escapes customary definition : because he runs off known lines, hewing new paths of thought ; and he aggravates settled minds all the more by his insistence that thought is not enough, that it is but a call to action.

In any one of the diverse subjects he has mastered and added to, he annoys the specialist in that particular field : reporters of the Press at his first demonstration of the Charting of Life (and even at his lectures too, generally) lay down their pens saying, " We can't report this stuff." He even eludes the few who try to follow him.

" People want," he once blazed out to me, " to put me into one of their pigeon-holes ; but you see I put most of them into one of mine instead ; namely, into that of the Past ! "

And to a journalist who came to him, demanding an all inclusive headline by which to describe him, he flared round—fixing him with piercing eyes like stilettos :

" Deliver the label means deliver the

[1] *British Medical Journal.*
[2] Lewis Mumford—see *The Interpreter.*

74

" Bunkum ! " he cried. " Am I a Darwinian
or a Spencerian, a Ruskinian or Carlylean, an
Aristotelian or a Platonist, a Socratean or a
Pythagorean, a Buddhist, Hindu, or a Parsee,
a Bahaist or a Theosophist, a Jew, a Druid, a
Chaldean, or an Egyptian ; a Roman Catholic
or any sort of a Protestant, a Deist, Agnostic,
a Positivist or an Atheist, a Freudian or a
Jungian, a Bergsonian, Nietzschian—or, if you
like, a Smithsonian ! Am I an Imperialist,
or a Home Ruler, a Nationalist or a Sinn
Feiner, a Liberal or a Conservative, a Tory or a
Revolutionary, a Co-operator or a Socialist, an
Anarchist or a Syndicalist, a Tolstoyian or a
Bolshevik ?—and my answer is, emphatically—
' Yes, of course ! ' "[1]

And then he promptly puts all these labels
in his pigeon-hole of the Past, with the
remark :

" Every man who really and fairly thinks
over all these doctrines must go so far with
them and see some truth in each. For we are
heirs of all the ages, even our own ! People
are never entirely fools ; and there must be
some good in all specialisms, some reality
somewhere in each one ; some vision, some
glimpse of fact at least ; and I try to find that
and profit by it, especially as, in so far as all
these types of people are mostly still living
(or preserved !) there must be some good in

[1] *The Interpreter.*

75

them, h'm ?   For else they couldn't have
survived ! "
"My advice to writers is," he added, as he
reached for his shabby, out-of-date, hat and
darted off to keep an appointment with the
Governor of Jerusalem, "always steal from
everyone. How's that for a headline, eh ? "
It was quite like the cricketer's "How's
that ! " His listener was bowled out. Small
wonder that the crumpled journalist, like one
who has met a whirlwind, collected his scattered
notes, and, to do him justice, went off, scratch-
ing his head, to write an article which his
editor threw down and which no paper would
publish ! For newspapers, too, have their
obsolete card-indexes: each column in each page
is allotted to certain subjects. There is little
space in a newspaper for an obscure Dundee
professor of botany "who takes all knowledge
as his province in order to harness it to life."[1]
To be fair, though, in this last year the
press of the world has given space to him and
has done its best to form an opinion of him—
an opinion unanimously enthusiastic —but not
one has understood his "Charting of Life. This
still baffles the best of them. Only in India
has even an effort been made to describe
those diagrams, which, to Kipling,[2] seem to
suggest the Kabballa.

[1] *Manchester Guardian* and *New York Times*.
[2] In a private letter to me.

GEDDES

As time goes on, and in every country, we find these things are, a little at a time, slowly but surely being realized ; and, what is more, applied in phases of everyday life.

But to reach the public at large we next come up against the booksellers—and these, too, have their out-of-date catalogue-system, their obsolete card indexes—outside things as they are !

But Bose once said to me of his own books, with characteristic resignation, " My books are read by the few who care for them ". And so, little by little, the influence of such men spreads like a wireless whisper over the entire world—for thought has no frontiers and its progress cannot be for ever stopped by card index boundaries or the apathy of the canned, the preserved, or the pigeon-holed !

Geddes has published some thirty books, including town planning reports, often large; several books written in collaboration with colleagues — Branford and Arthur Thomson especially. Yet to-day he says he is no writer, complains of his " life-long silence "—meaning with the pen—and he never has believed very much in the writing of books. He has always written under protest.

For over fifty years he has talked ceaselessly to all and sundry, in Scotland, England, France, Belgium, Germany, Cyprus, Mexico, India, America and Palestine.

77

From whence comes this marvellous fertility, this almost terrifying flow of energy, this vigorous clarity of thought, this unusual persistence of endeavour, and this unprecedented coupling of thought with action—of Dreams and Deeds ? (For he never rests until he has personally carried a theory to its application in actual life.)

What impulse drives him on to this creative fever—this passion for Work — Experience— Ideas — Synthesis ; Folk — Feeling—Emotion —Polity ; Place—Sense—Imagery—Achieve - ment ?[1]

Can the Freudian psycho-analyst account for it by the one word : " Sublimation " ? Is it the result of Environment ? Is it the outcome of Heredity ? Can it be labelled as a Sport of Nature ? Is it all these taken together ?

We come back to wonder if material forces alone can account for one man taking the world in his hands, and, like Michael Angelo with a piece of rough-hewn marble, like Hernandez with an unformed slab of iron-hard Diorite, attempt to reshape it himself till it shall correspond to some vision seen with his mind's eye ?

" I do not know enough to profess the science of God ", Geddes said quietly when questioned about religion ; and he would be the last

[1] See " Charting of Life " in *The Interpreter*.

78

person to allow any analysis of himself to be mixed up with the Church Theory of the Supernatural—the reality of which he would, however, not take upon himself to deny. "Maybe . . . Maybe . . ." would be all he would allow himself to say, for here is his boundary, he is a man of modern science and not a theologian. And since no accurate scientific law has been found to account for the impulse which moves such men, he would simply state " Science does not know and cannot say ".

He once described himself : " I'm an old Bull of the Herd ", with a swift smile and a chuckle, and with the inevitable query at the end, which characterises so many of his summaries—" H'm ? " and then the waiting for his listener's reply. Another time he drew a different self-portrait in a line : " I'm the boy that rings the bell and runs away ! " Still, in all this there is something inherited. His father was a long-lived captain in the renowned Royal Highlanders, and " in all Perth there was no man who so arrested and held public estimation ·and esteem . . . The very embodiment of a good Soldier of the Master ".[1]

There is something of environment in it too, for Geddes' patriotic love of Scotland is akin to Bose's passion for India. Wherever Geddes has been—all over the world—he has taken

[1] James Macdonald, *Bailie of Linlithgow*, written for *The Interpreter*.

79

Scotland with him; and in his old-age, at the meeting-place of East and West, at Montpellier, in Southern France, he has revived the spirit of that medieval Scots College in Paris, which tradition claims to have helped towards the foundation of the Paris university before Oxford was thought of. In the College des Ecossais, Plan des Quatre Seigneurs, Montpellier, his creative energy and conservative, yet constructive, instinct have again found outlet; and here he has built what must become his own Memorial upon the city's nearest hill.

There is a movement on foot to acquire for British Youth for ever this College des Ecossais, into the planning of which Geddes is putting his best educational ideas; and, says Professor Arthur Thomson, he is " the most educative person I have known, the most thought stimulating man I have ever met—he introduces order into one's thinking, but it is dynamic order. He makes one go on . . . a maker of intellectual roads, opening up paths of thought and work, giving vistas that last for life ".[1]

As a boy, from his very earliest days, he was in a foremost outstanding rank all his own; active alike in mathematics and modern languages, in chemistry and in nature studies, geological and botanical; so above all, a rambler

[1] See Prof. J. Arthur Thomson in *The Interpreter*.

GEDDES

exploring both nature and history over the
Perth region.

His father built him a little laboratory and
workshop, so he became something alike of
chemist and carpenter ; a skilled craftsman ;
he went into the National Bank of Perth for a
year and more and learnt something of business and finance. Then he went to the School
of Mines in London, as a scientific student, and
became an assistant first to Huxley, and then
to Schafer and Burdon Sanderson at University
College. After that, one university did not
satisfy him—he prospected in Oxford *and* in
Cambridge, but was more attracted to Con-
tinental Universities. Like a medieval student
he has wandered over Europe, discovering
for himself the teachers at whose feet he wished
to learn ; thus he first found his spiritual and
intellectual home in the University of Paris,
and largely also in the University of Montpellier, which is at once much of Oxford and
of Edinburgh for France, and from earliest
times, one of the leading Schools of Medicine
in Europe.

Yet his student life was not wholly lived in
universities. After working largely at marine
zoological stations, he went on an expedition
to Mexico, digging fossils, searching woods and
pools, and rejoicing in natural beauty above
all. But, as in many lives, here came the
crisis which might have " finished " him ; for

81

now he went nearly blind (blindness has been in his family on his mother's side). " What is a visual to do when he goes blind ? I had to ask myself," he wrote in later life ; " one day, feeling over my darkened window-panes " (confined as he was to a dark room for many weeks) " there came the idea — make graphics ! "[1]

And from this initial inspiration has gradually come the whole of his Calculus, his Charting of Life, and many other Notations, and Paths of Thought ; and these have developed into his designs for gardens, universities, cities, and for general regional planning—indeed, his Etho-Polity itself. Out of the dark came the light : his eyesight recovered, and he started upon a new life. He has never been more than a part-time professor—for, while teaching in various universities from Edinburgh to Bombay, and, in the interval, for nearly forty years Professor of Botany at University College, Dundee, he always refused the year's appointment income and took only a third of it, preferring thus to limit his income and to profess each year for only one term out of the three—for was not this the price of freedom ? He had the full approval of his life-long and most devoted colleague, Mrs. Geddes. Few men, not in possession of a private fortune, could afford to sacrifice

[1] *The Interpreter.*

GEDDES

two-thirds of their professional income every
year, and few wives and children would so
cordially accept it ! Yet they managed to
provide a delightful, even ideal, home on the
top of the Castle Hill in Old Edinburgh, and
to give to each of their three children an
education which fitted them for life. The
family was at once free and united, and all
were willing that the breadwinner should give
up most of his year in the pursuit of ideas and
projects in which they had faith.

To his University colleagues, however, he
appeared something of a truant—who ran
about the world and only returned in summer
time. Also—as a rather feared person who
had, with his friend J. Arthur Thomson, as
early as 1889 (when the subject was entirely
taboo !) published a book on " The Evolution
of Sex "—a book, by the way, not yet out of
date, as the recent, summarized and developed
version of it—" Sex " (Home University
Library), and its companions, " Evolution "
and " Biology " by the same authors, will
show.

And it is perhaps only natural that " specialized scientists probably look upon Geddes in
the same way as his brethren must regard a
monk who has left the cloister ".[1]

They could not realize that he left the cloister
only to carry its gospel into the world, and to

[1] *The Scientific Worker.*

83

return to it periodically for needed refreshment and re-inspiration, bringing with him experience of Work, Folk and Place with which to develop his Ideas, Doctrines, and Images ; many of which were next applied in experimental life. To many, of course, his thoughts and theories have seemed mere " Dreams," but these he has used to feed further vision and collate further facts to hurl out into the world of Deeds again. For to him the world is a rotating " swastika " of Acts—Facts—Thoughts—Deeds—each being ineffective, indeed sterile, without the other, for the four are One—in Life.

So it came about that his books were read, his lectures attended, only by the few, and these sometimes learned men, sometimes simple student women, but with sympathy and insight alike. But—" where two or three are gathered together "—by means of these few it has come about that in well nigh every city and university of the world to-day there are at least one or two sowers of his seed, and it is such sowing which is eventually cumulative and which slowly grows in force. To-day there is scarcely a school or college or even a Government Department, where at least one or two of his ideas are not penetrating—quite anonymously, of course !

A man and his family may economise and sacrifice and treat offers of higher pay for more

ordinary work with contempt—on the quest
of the Holy Grail. Yet, for the application
of scientific work, money is a necessity. Less
fortunate than Bose, there have never been
Societies or Governments offering grants or
endowments to Geddes. He has covered too
wide an area to appeal, up to now, even to the
Rockefeller Foundation. But his work has
not lacked its friends: and the undertakings
he has founded, or helped to found, still go on ;
they have more often needed to be helped
financially by himself than able to pay for
any work he might do for them—yet, though
the pinch has often been severe, the fact remains that his work, however often delayed,
has never come to a stop.

Even in the War, his " Cities and Town
Planning Exhibition " (the priceless collection
of many years) was sunk in the Indian Ocean
by the famous " Emden." On this, an artist
in New York, who had never seen him, wrote
an article about this loss, and called it " The
Destruction of the Future ". Nothing seemed
to be done about it beyond a brief paragraph
in one or two London papers, and some of
those who knew him least said to each other,
" This will be the end of Geddes ". Yet,
within three months, almost anonymously,
one here and one there, of those who put their
faith in him, managed to form and send out
to him in India a new collection, in some ways

even superior to the one which War-Vandalism had destroyed. His Town Planning Exhibition thus went on, and through the main capitals of India.

The thing which did nearly break him was not connected with his work at all, but with his feelings. Geddes is a man of deep friendships and strong emotions; so of family affection correspondingly.

In a few weeks in 1917 he lost his beloved wife by fever, and their adored eldest son in battle—both in the service of their country. Mrs. Geddes in India, where she was organising and working with him; Alasdair, after winning the M.C. and the Legion of Honour as " the ace of the balloons," and being spoken of as " the best Observer in the British Army," in France. It was then that the understanding friendship of Sir Jagadis and Lady Bose and other Indian friends, managed to save a man well nigh broken-hearted and crushed. Happily he was with them for the summer at Darjeeling—a glorious place of meditation in the mountains; and gradually, very gradually, Nature and Time did their healing work. Geddes returned to the battlefield of life once more—armed more than ever to combat the ignorance which had destroyed almost all that he loved, more ferocious than before in argument; and, as many could see, with less of physical strength left—yet mentally more determined than ever.

GEDDES

Before, he had been a man with a vocation :
now, he became a man with a mission ; though
even while writing this I fear to bring down his
wrath upon my head for using such words.

Someone once called him " genius ". " Stuff
and nonsense," he thundered savagely, " I
merely work harder than most of you—and I
daresay," he added with quick forgiveness,
" I have more than the average amount of
physical health and strength."

There is nothing abnormal about genius, in
his opinion, though he will not let the word
be applied to himself. " The biggest flower
on this rhododendron head," he pointed out
to me one day, taking the cluster in his hand
gently, " is the most normal flower—the rest
are a little sub-normal, that is all " ; and left
me to draw my inference as to his suggestion
of applying this to society. For he is ever
elusive, and he always leaves his friends to
draw their own conclusions. You can't pin
him down ; with his skeleton keys he picks
the lock—and is gone. " Obviously it is his
architectural faculty that has saved him ;
there stand the places he has built—visible,
tangible, delectable ; concrete proof that he is
no mere visionary ".[1] But " he lives at high
altitudes and when he lifts his friends up they
suffer from mountain sickness ".[2]

[1] *Without Prejudice*, by the late Israel Zangwill (Heine-
mann, 1895). Quoted in *The Interpreter*.
[2] Prof. Arthur Thomson in *The Interpreter*.

PIONEERS OF SCIENCE

There seems to be in these pioneers of science an inherent spirit of poetry. Sir Ronald Ross writes his poems and even publishes them; Bose writes and speaks poetic prose; with Geddes all is Drama (is he a Celt for nothing?). But, go to a flower-show with him, and you will find him outstrip the very poets themselves! All poetry is clearly not in the writing of it.

The best of his writing, where he covers all subjects, from drainage to religion, and from all sciences to most arts, may be found in his "Report to the Durbar of Indore",[1] which is a masterpiece of concentration and clarity.

"These marvellous volumes constitute a complete Geddesian Gospel, in which the financial and statistical details, while they would satisfy the veriest Dry-as-Dust, are illumined by a noble idealism to which in turn they give substance: eloquent . . . The overwhelming effect of them is due to this almost unique combination of the practical with the religious . . . I know of no such transfusion of the practical by the spiritual, strange as it is to come upon it in this professional report of an architect ".[2]

Geddes is nothing if not witty and a French writer has compared him, in this, to Bernard Shaw: he is ever twinkling with suppressed fun, and never more so than when he has to

[1] 2 vols. Batsford.

[2] The late Israel Zangwill. Introduction to *The Interpreter*.

GEDDES

interview officials. His wit is often biting,
sometimes bitter, but always scintillating.
His mingling of jest with seriousness was best
seen when he got an Indian Prince to let him
take his place as Maharajah for a day!

This great game, played with royal approval
and official sanction, even active help, he now
tells of with the highest glee—like a boy describing a prank!

Given full powers and being absolute
monarch he staged and himself headed, riding
on a richly caparisoned elephant, a great
procession, such as the Maharajahs have in
India and which, therefore, the masses understand.

But this one was done with a different purpose—a huge joke indeed, but one with the
most serious civic endeavour. For by this
pageant—a dramatization of nature and citizen-
ship, and thus applied Sociology—he under-
took to win the people to share in city improve-
ment and rid their city of the Plague![1]

The people have called him, ever after,
" The old Sahib who charmed away the
plague ". He had succeeded, where other
methods had failed!

" Patrick Geddes comes like a Crusader
. . . to bring the world out of its dusty pigeon-
holes . . . His talk envelops you like an
atmosphere, your mind becomes all windows

[1] See his *Report to the Durbar of Indore* (Batsford, 2 vols.).

into the past and windows into the future. Learning and life are no longer divorced, but going hand in hand to complete triumph over the misery and confusion of things . . . There are dozens of reputations to-day which owe their inspiration to Geddes, just as there are movements and ideas, unassociated with his name, that truly belong to him ".[1]

This is the man who, after the war, was chosen as designer of the Hebrew University in Jerusalem, and who has also done much Town Planning for Palestine, at Haifa, Tel-a-viv and Jerusalem.

At times one thinks of him like a shepherd, wrapped in silence on some distant hill, alone with his Muse ; at other times one pictures him as a chieftain, gathering his scattered clan for the final battle against the confusion of things as they are ; and if necessary dying in the fight for things as they scientifically and ideally ought to be !

[1] *The Pillars of Society*, by A. G. Gardiner (Nisbet), quoted in *The Interpreter*.

CHAPTER III

BRANFORD

" A King is not saved by the multitude of a host ;
A mighty man is not delivered by great strength ".
Psalm 33, 16.
(Jewish version)

IN the primeval forest great fires arise ; a spark from a passing steamer, a match thoughtlessly thrown down, work devastation for many miles, to all that grows, and to the animals and people who inhabit the forest. Blown by the wind, flames turn the tall forest into a burning furnace, issuing blinding smoke and obscuring vision over the miles of width of the mighty river below. Yet such fires fertilize the soil. Even more than the fanning wind may the moss carry fire : for in these forests there often lies a combustible soil, and with it runs the glowing fire. Man has no power over primeval forest fire—except to start it. What man starts he is often powerless to extinguish. The seasons and the elements are beyond the grasp of humankind.

" Come behold the works of the Lord
Who hath made desolations in the earth.
He maketh wars to cease unto the end of the earth,
He breaketh the bow, and cutteth the spear asunder.
Let be and know that I am God ".[1]

[1] Psalm 46, 9, 10 (Jewish version).

Behind the School of British Sociology, guiding it at once in the field of exact science and of deepening insight—detached, inextinguishable—sits a small, thin, worn man, fingering his fragile pointed beard, biting, between hatchet-hard lips, his frail moustache. Grey in complexion and with faintly reddish hair turning grey ; the image of suppressed nervous energy hidden beneath a shy, abrupt manner ; biting the ends of his clipped words as he talks with restrained emotion, his words—brief, sudden—are to the point.

This man has eyes which contradict the first impression of his exterior appearance. They pierce, they are alert, they dart out fire ; at times they blaze fiercely, at times they shine. They might be the eyes of a saint ; at times they might be the eyes of a fanatic. Yet they are surely the eyes of a friend. Though they curtain fires which burn through eternity, yet they are kinder than the fire, gentler than the fanning wind.

There is humour, too, in these eyes, which belie the hard-headedness that is often so characteristic of their owner. The first thing that strikes you—those darting, alert, sad eyes—mirror of a disembodied spirit—are also the last thing you remember about Victor Branford. They are eyes which will never grow old : they are emblems of a spirit which will not be killed.

Here is a financier to whom the jingling of coins is merely an accompaniment to the orches-tration of ideas. Here is a man, fired with a mission from early youth, who has never ceased to battle, banner in hand, towards the Holy Grail.

His self-imposed mission is to bring the ends of the earth together : for he, too, sees a vision of unity ; he grasps religion in one hand and science in the other, and determines the two shall be made one with practical life, and even with finance !

In his later years he publishes his *Science and Sanctity*, which, solacing and inspiring to the few, has as yet made no impression on the multitude.

His laboratory is enclosed in his head : his medium is Thought : he has literary gift enough to express himself, but his style is not modern : it is sometimes too close-packed to be even clear : he is not a writer who can easily move people : he is not one who can carry them away. He comes of a Puritan race, over-disciplined, restrained, reserved to the *n*th degree ; and he cannot give literary vent to the fires which consume him, neither is he eloquent in speech. A very disillusioned pioneer, he nevertheless ceaselessly " carries on ", deathless in his loyalty.

Not only his life, but his fortune, he em-barked upon his sociological venture. Yet neither for his ideas nor for himself has he won much of a following, nor any degree of popularity. Reserved as a hermit in his cave, venturing out, he has driven his chariot, harnessed to a star, regardless of consequences. By nature he shuns popularity—his workplaces have been the counting-house and the study by turns. Like the soil in the forest which carries on the fire underground, Branford works quietly and the result of his work is not lost ; it is traversing the continents.

British Sociology, of which he is a main leader, and the *Sociological Review*, of which he is Editor, are thought by many competent judges to be the sanest, the most scientific, the most traditional and the most evolutionary of such movements in the world.

Editor of books, mostly published at his own expense, he has collected in *The Making of the Future* Series (edited by himself and Patrick Geddes) thoughts which might otherwise have remained unheard—his own contribution to this and other series being not less valuable than those of his colleagues.

In the face of apathy and ignorance, he has persisted, and now, no longer young, he persists still. A knight of the burning pestle—a very valiant knight—he has triumphed over his own delicate physique.

In early manhood he occupied the library of his predecessor who had died of consumption.

The germs of this terrible disease were in the books, and attacked him. He determined not to die of consumption and, though in danger of it all his life, he managed to keep it at bay.

Late in life he married Sybella Gurney, of ancient Quaker stock, a sociologist, devoting herself to the study of village folk and their problems, who threw herself, and to a large extent, her fortune, into the work of the town-planning and garden city movement, and also that of the Sociological Society, in the high endeavour to formulate and spread that Etho-Polity, that Ideal of the City, which is at once the root and flower of the thinking of their leader—Patrick Geddes—for the betterment of world (and village) conditions and government.

Childless, this couple adopted two infant boys, to bring them up in the Geddes and Branford ideas of education and development.

Of the books written in collaboration by the Editor of the *Making of the Future* series, the *Coming Polity* has had the most influence, and is now in its second edition : it was of this book that the " Times Literary Supplement " wrote :—

" Every chapter is an act of faith, a venture of the Spirit through the darkness of the future, grasping at things as yet unrealised ! "

What has urged this fragile, delicate man of

business, financially comfortable, to take up such strenuous adventures ?

Shy and retiring, it certainly was not ambition that moved him. Was the spark which started the blaze within him that of his friendship with Geddes, Arthur Thomson and other idealists in his college days at Edinburgh ? And was it not also a strong abstract interest— the appeal of Ideas ?

Certainly this man, at first sight as dry-as-dust in outward appearance (but for his eyes), is at heart a poet : has he not sociologized the saints and discovered their life-secret to be that they were simply poets living their poetry ?[1]

I think in his little white vellum-covered book, St. Columba, published by Patrick Geddes and Colleagues (for Geddes has long been a publisher too) Branford has put more of himself than in any other thing he has done. If this was the trend of his nature, he did not let it contain him : stern self-discipline is written in every line of his face and figure. From his mental cloister he forced himself to contend with ideas at war. And what the Fabian Society, led by Sydney Webb and Bernard Shaw, has been for the last thirty or forty years, in English politics, Branford's Sociological Society, with its Regional Association and kindred activities, will be during the

[1] St. Columba, by Victor Branford, M.A.

BRANFORD

generation now opening; and an influence even on the policies of nations in the opening future.

Here indeed is another part of his Mission, to think out the ways and means for the financing of the Coming Polity. His is, largely, the golden background upon which his picture of the future is being slowly painted : and all over the world there are now pioneers, few but virile, laying in the groundwork of the vision to which he has sworn loyalty. His message is " Eutopia and how to pay for it."[1] It was in a crisis of civilization, not unlike the present, that Sir Thomas More wrote his *Utopia*, and in its title punned between Outopea, meaning nowhere, and Eutopia, meaning the good place.

Geddes and Branford have never hesitated to proclaim Eutopia as realizable here and now increasingly ; they invoke in its service the best possible use of all the resources available, physical, mental and moral.[2] Their problem ? —how to search out in the life around them the best of the past, and thus find material wherewith to fashion their ideal of the future :[2] hence they proclaim : " As you explore the ways of Eutopia you rediscover the best of our social inheritance."

Taking the question of health, they have been pushing on from physiology into psy-

[1] *Our Social Inheritance*, by Geddes and Branford (LePlay House Press.)
[2] *Our Social Inheritance.*

97

chology (long before this became fashionable with leading doctors) ; and thus they have influenced medical as well as social thinkers and teachers. In the coupling of these two sciences Branford and Geddes have been pioneers : but when to this religion[1] was added (especially by the former), is it any wonder this combination shook the conventions of the specialized professions ? Such combinations are not popular.

Like the saints of old, but now on a scientific basis, Branford stands for resistance to temptations ; and this not merely in a negative sense, but for spiritual achievement, so that psychic and creative purpose may come into man's interplay with environment,[1] and this not only for individuals, but for groups and communities, cities and nations.

This is a pioneer who has lived to see the ideas for which he has worked slowly yet increasingly coming to the front. His mass of writings on Civics are more and more occupied by the things of the spirit ; so that the modern science of Civics, largely inaugurated at Le Play House, and in the Sociological Society, is approaching in grasp and insight the truth of the Psalmist who wrote : " Except the Ideal build the City, the watchman worketh but in vain."[1] By such efforts, treated and made more possible by Branford, the best of

[1] *Our Social Inheritance.*

our modern youth in great cities is being led back to—and may they one day take, as part of early education—that oath of the Athenian Youth, which he recommends to Boy Scouts to-day :—" We will never disgrace this, our city, by any act of dishonesty or cowardice, nor ever desert our suffering comrades in the ranks—we will fight for the ideals and sacred things of the City, both alone and with many. . . . Thus in all ways we will transmit this city, not only not less, but greater, better and more beautiful than it was transmitted to us."[1]

This is the new patriotism served by Branford.

But to take an oath is not enough : it has to be carried into action ; and every application of science has to be financed. This is not to say that it shall be " commercialized," or that it need deteriorate in application. It is not a question of exploiting a patent, for there is no law for the protection of ideas. Branford applies his ideas to the modern Credit-System, which, while it is at present the weakness of the Machine Industry, is nevertheless one of the vastest of economic organizations,[1] and can be used on ideal lines. " The whole handling of money imparts a corresponding habit of mind."[2]

[1] *Our Social Inheritance.*
[2] *The Drift of Revolution,* by Victor Branford, " Papers for the Present ", No. 9 (LePlay House Press).

PIONEERS OF SCIENCE

" *The social education of the banker*," Branford is convinced, " *in the control of credit is thus on the first plane of national need.*" But to accomplish this education, the people, too, must be educated in the right handling of money. The credit system must be used for a deliberately planned social purpose. This system draws its fundamental life-source from the working classes. Its right use is the banker's technical problem—and he has grown accustomed to think of public wealth in terms of debt.[1] The first change needed is to alter this habit of mind.

A modest portion of his energies must be diverted (and as soon as may be) from conventional " business enterprise," and devoted to City-planning. For this means to set about the production of real wealth—indeed that and most essential of all, in the present house-famine of our cities—and to adapt the cheque and clearing-house system to this and kindred wealth-producing activities. Branford thinks of wealth in terms of growing possession of things necessary and useful to life, rather than in mere money terms of coins or stocks and shares ; and so he sees the possibility of genuine civic investment remunerative in the realities of life. The city is thus discerned and thought of in terms of its fundamental

[1] *The Banker's Part in Reconstruction*, by Victor Branford, " Papers for the Present ", No. 2.

needs, of homes and gardens, of household
goods and food products, rather than merely
as a conglomeration of counting houses in
" the City " and overcrowded dormitories
anywhere beyond.

Branford's mission is thus to persuade the
Bankers and their associated activities to come
out of their " thought-cages," and to realize
that Eutopia can be made to pay! For one
thing, this will put an end to mere embittered
evolutionary struggles.

" Long overdue," he proclaims, " is this
extension of the credit system," and in various
papers he works out with technical clearness,
the needed developments for this extension of
that present credit system, which, to him, is
already one of the masterpieces of modern
times. How to apply this invention to the
service of the city—and thus of mankind ?—
he asks continually.

In the deepest and most practical sense he
strives to bring Temporal and Spiritual powers
and agencies together, and thus to capitalize
a greater fund of creative energy than is yet
being conserved while these two are left to go
on functioning separately as at present.
Apply the science of Sociology to arouse the
mind of the financier ; in this way true progress, for the bettering of human living and
working conditions, coincident with the accum-
ulation of " improved " property (real capital),

ever increasing in true value, will result.
There is, in all this, nothing visionary—it is
simply evolution in the method of handling
money, the details of which he has worked out
on a business basis.

And so he stands upon a new field, combining Science and Finance, in all its multifarious
workings ; and all in a unifying spirit, truly
social and moral, and thus in the deepest sense
religious. This, of course, leads him to his
" Third Alternative " (a political alternative
to revolution and reaction), from which is
growing up a new and vigorous theory of politics, likely in fifty years' time to transform the
present party machines, and to ring the death-
knell of mere present-day Conservatives,
Liberals, and of vague and revolutionary
Socialisms alike.

Are these the vague prophesyings of a
visionary allowing himself mere flights of
imagination ?

Is it likely that a successful man who has
been all his life in the business world, financing
and directing railways, and with a lifelong
training in and experience of the workings
of finance, should publicly make a fool of
himself ?

*Is it not, rather, that here we have the thoughtful
financier pioneering ahead of his times ?* Over-
stepping the conventions of the business
world ? Diverting the course of an organiza-

tion become a stereotyped routine ? And, as the ideas and methods of Geddes in education are gradually penetrating the Schools and Universities ; as the methods of Bose in research are now accepted by the very scientists who once turned their backs on him ; so, though with even more difficulty, the financial methods of Branford must, in due time, be accepted. This, in short, becomes no less than *progress-in-evolution-within-the-Banks*.

An expert in finance, with Branford's energy, had personal gain been his life-motif, might have become a multi-millionaire. He could then, like Carnegie, Rockefeller, and others, have given away millions in charity or philanthropic enterprises.

But these others belonged to an era that is coming to a close : Branford belongs to the Awakening Future. He has seen that with all their generous giving, beneficial though it is, these individual millionaires can do little. Their millions are swallowed up—and the bad conditions remain.

Past master in the technique of finance, Branford saw early that Socialistic economics were as useless for lasting benefit as have been the old individualistic economics of the capitalists. Before Russia demonstrated in practice the flaw in Fabian Finance, he had prepared his Third Alternative.

He stands for Evolution in the methods of handling money, for a re-vision of banking technique ; and so with his clear vision and guidance a new way opens for financial enterprise.

Small wonder, one man taking up arms against the vast and well-entrenched army of established finance, that his appearance is dry, and his lips are set like iron ! He battles on—undismayed—certain that individualism is of the past, that communism is not practical, that the present system is crashing, and that in the logical development of contemporary social evolution—from which the financier is not more immune than any one of us—the Third Alternative (discovered and elucidated by him) will come into practical application. The old card-indexes cannot be re-arranged in a day : to attempt this would bring chaos, as surely as Kapec's " Kaburetor "[1] brought his world to ruin.

But in course of time conventions decay : and as, slowly and one by one, they disintegrate, so idea upon idea can be inserted till the whole system shall become changed—for Science cannot in the long run be denied entrance to the doors of the Banks.

As the old leaves fall off the trees, nature is providing for the new leaves which, after the winter's rest-period, will take their place in

[1] See *The Kaburetor*, by K. Kapec.

the exuberance of spring, when life is renewed.
Even in the mind of banking this seasonal
growth is going on unperceived. The old
Bankers die off : and as the new ones are being
prepared, new ideas are slowly coming, with
them, into Power. The University of the
Future is preparing the Finance of the Future,
and it is not for nothing that the eyes of Victor
Branford glow. The spark he has kindled
will not die out. In this faith he lives, and
works on.

Consider, too, his interpretation and criticism of the old system. " The inventors and
masters of the Industrial Revolution, the
manufacturers and merchants of the eighteenth
century, the bankers and financiers of the
nineteenth, were in considerable preponder-
ançe members of the Nonconformist Churches
. . . their Theology chilled and settled into
their Political Economy." He reads the story
of the past, with its hopes, endeavours and
failures, in his " Westminster : a City Survey
for disoriented citizens."[1] For, in a very real
sense, their city is at once the school and the
university of each community ; and the
history of its civilization, with a forecast of its
failure, may be made from such a city-survey.

Not to run on too fast, I come to a standstill
as a line in one of his books reminds me that
the Royal Society still boycotts Sociology,

[1] *Our Social Inheritance.*

which, though its foundations were laid a century ago by Comte, to be developed in England by (notably) Herbert Spencer, has not yet received official recognition as a Science by our learned societies or even by our universities to any adequate extent.

Psychology is also taboo to the " scientific pundits. In what it fails to do, as well in what it does, the science of Burlington House thus exercises a deep and far-reaching influence, first in practical obscurantism in these studies, but also in the false perspective in which the physical sciences stand, so long as they leave out these higher ones."[1]

But that the Royal Society can be converted by time and patient persistence, Bose has proved during his own lifetime. These blocks, in the movement of ideas, whether in around Burlington House or the Bank of England, can be (like the fog which annually descends upon them), and are, being dispersed.

Financial problems are the most difficult of any ; but gradually, and as enlightenment comes through the schools and the universities, the tone of the Press will change. Fresh public opinion is all the time being formed, and the managers' offices and vaults of the banks cannot forever hold out against the intellectual advances and practical changes now in process. The introduction of the credit and clearing

[1] *Our Social Inheritance.*

system itself created a revolution in Banking
circles ; and the social extension of this, for
which Branford pleads, is by no means an
impossibility for the near future to achieve.

These future financiers are being educated
to-day. A gleam of the work of the pioneers
is finding its way into their training. Yet
still they are too much dominated by machine-
made science still unsocial. Current thought,
and in Britain especially,[1] is still essentially
pre-sociological, for almost all are still too
much " drilled throughout their best years in
the memorization of dead knowledge, and then
tested and measured as to fitness for national
service by their skill and facility in disgorging
the pellets of information with which they were
previously crammed."[1]

So we must wait till yet another generation
comes along. It took fifty years for Socialism,
based on the materialistic outlook of the nineteenth century, to come to power ; and years
have still to pass before Sociology as a science
is recognised officially, and perhaps even
longer before it can transform the Banks.

But even if it should take a whole century,
the year 2028 will see the Politics of the world
moved towards Branford's " Third Alternative " ; and the corresponding world-finance
will run on his " social extension of the credit-
system." With all this, too, there is coming

[1] *Our Social Inheritance.*

107

the de-commercializing of the pleasures of the people, with deep influence upon occupations accordingly, indeed an economic metamorphosis.

Our great-grandchildren will not know the meaning of " The ˙ Commercial Theatre " ; for with the extension of the credit system will come a better method of handling the Arts which are the Eye and the Ear of the City of the Future—no less than they were the expression of the City Beautiful of the past—when Religion, Art and Science were at one.

A part of the dream of Branford therefore lies, logically, in the Eugenic Theatre,[1] in which adolescence, with its quests of life and love, shall be frankly expressed, *but also idealised*, and in close touch with the scientific life of the period, and its renewing idealism, truly religious.

" Acknowledgment of Sex ", which he sees in the Greek Theatre " as the fundamental force, at once of high personality and of social progress (and not, as in our present-day theatre, as degenerate) will be the corner-stone of the theatre of the future, for ' who shapes the dream, decides the deed ', and the theatre is not only the mirror of, but is mirrored in, society. The Greeks ", he continues, " if

[1] *Interpretations and Forecasts,* by Victor Branford (Duckworth).

they were ignorant of the doctrine of descent
by natural selection, at least promoted the
practice of ascent by epic selection—the young
Athenians were taken to the Theatre to learn
the types of personality to imitate—and to
avoid ".[1]

And on this classic model Branford builds
up the future. " Let the Arts of the University combine in her service with the Crafts
of the City ",[1] he cries. " The continuing
co-operation of all these and many others
there must be if religion is to be maintained as
a working faith ". " The age of ascent by
epic selection is not finished, maybe it is hardly
yet begun."

Why the " Eugenic " Theatre ?

Because, as even before the war I heard
Dr. Saleeby prove, Shakespeare (and the
Greeks no less) was, like all the poets, an un-
conscious eugenist.

Branford knows that the poetic impulse
exists to-day in the life around us ; and that
knowledge is accumulating daily, merely await-
ing the poet who will dramatize it. With the
advent of such a poet the Theatre will live
again, and be the very centre of the educational stimulus of every city : for the best
part (and the worst) of a people's education
lies in its pleasures. The worst sign of the
present times is the perpetual commercializa-

[1] *Interpretations and Forecasts.*

tion of our pleasures, with its lowering of the standard on all sides.

In the awakening future, Bank—City—Theatre will be at One, and the Temple will interleave this manifold book of Life. For the Church, too, will be extended.

Like Geddes and Bose, Branford is breaking down the barriers between the old customary pigeon-holes. Students of Sociology will grow up into captains of industry, and these into Directors of Theatres and organizers of extended religion. For he sees " The City at its best, as has sometimes been achieved, is a confederation of artificers, artists, statesmen and prophets, united by the heroic urge of creating a milieu out of their own mental imagery ", and he thinks the rarity of this achievement is because " Human bees have such a wealth of imagery for the cells, such a poverty of plans for the hive ".

And so he charts out boldly the technique needed for the financing of the needed plans ; for these develop into City designs, including a-programme for revised and revitalized Work, Pleasure, Education, and Government. This developing from his doctrine of " the social heritage." For we hold within us, as our social inheritance, the latent possibilities for a future equal to our highest dreams : and the will to achievement will not always be lacking. The Civic future, then, and the financing of it, are being at once soberly thought out in business terms, and yet also " flashed into unity in the ecstasies of vision ".[1]

Behind the movement towards The Coming Polity sits this frail-bodied pioneer in finance striving to embody his financial dream whereby the Civic Statesman shall be enabled to save the world from degeneration, finding the way to pay for the making of beauty and order out of surrounding chaos ! He is proving that the utilization of the natural and social sciences for the progress of the State-in-Evolution is indeed sound business ; for by it, and by no other means, is it possible to do away with the burden of debt and develop real wealth.

And so Victor Branford, with his glowing eyes, is quietly lighting the spark which shall illuminate the present banking system, and preparing the way for the great building up— in which the Banks have so large a part to play—of a better social life.

Not to destroy, but to fulfil, is thus his mission.

[1] *Interpretations and Forecasts.*

CHAPTER IV

ROERICH

" *It is hard for us to go on amidst the crowd,*
There are so many hostile forces and contrary wills !
. . . .
We shall sit down,
The crowd will pass on.

. . . .
We shall sit and wait.
If the tiding comes that sacred signs have appeared,
We shall struggle on.
If they be carried
We shall stand up and render homage.

. . . .
We shall come forth,—
When the time is ripe ".

(From the Russian) N. R

THE WORK

WHAT is there different in their natures that makes a man, in these days, to be an artist on the one hand or a scientist on the other ?

An artist and a scientist are two parts of a whole ; and in so far as, in modern times, a man becomes one *or* another, in so far is he but half of a man !

ROERICH

Like the scientist Humphry Davy, so the artist Nicholas Roerich writes poetry. But, as with Davy, so with him, writing is not enough.

Few people have noticed how much splitting up the Arts and Sciences of life came in with the discovery of the Atomic Theory—not consciously, but as though by some new instinct: possibly because the mass of modern knowledge seems beyond the capacity of any single person to completely master technically. The division is contemporary with the industrial Division of Labour.

Even Tagore is among those who carry this further; for in a letter to Roerich he wrote: "*Each art achieves its perfection when it opens for our mind the special gate whose key is in its exclusive possession. Truth is Infinite, but when I tried to find words to describe your pictures, I failed. It was because the language of words can only express a particular aspect of truth and the language of pictures finds its domain in truth where words have no access*"

All through this book I have been trying to carry analysis of character beyond the psycho-analysis fashionable to-day—because from the first it seemed to me no physical cause can explain all the issues which character involves. But concrete answers to my questions are often wanting: I can but throw

out suggestions for investigation : as when I
ask this question : What makes one man an
artist and another a scientist (since of old the
two were more often one), for both are urged
by the same original force, both contain in
themselves the same elements. Yet if I suddenly say the violet smells to one as it does
to the other, I come to a full stop. The first
whiff may smell as sweet to each ; the emotion
aroused may even be the same ; but the
scientist, even though he writes a poem on it,
will begin to wonder. He is not content to
feel and enjoy, not content to evolve out of
himself verses : his passion for enquiry begins.
Why has the violet its colour, whence comes its
scent ? I have seen the scientist take the blue
out of a violet and turn the violet pink ; and
take the pink out of the violet's purple, and
turn the flower blue ? Like a boy who takes
his toy to pieces, he *must* meddle with nature.
Leonardo was a meddler, too !

The artist, like the scientist, first exclaims
with joy. But he, too, begins an enquiry, only
it takes a different angle. He must record his
enjoyment, passionately express his sensation,
set down what he sees—even alter it to make
a design—for he, too, must meddle with nature,
re-arrange it. He, too, may, if it suits him,
turn the violet blue or pink, but only on his
canvas. He takes liberties with nature if it
suits his fancy so to do. He analyses it in its

114

environment, or in any new environment in which he may place it.

He, too, asks (?) He is as analytical as the scientist, but his first question is a different one. He sees that the violet is purple in certain lights and, as he knows that the variations possible in any given colour are infinite and cannot even all be seen by the human eye, he takes the colour of the violet as he finds it. But he analyses it in different lights, for he knows that colour, to the eye, is a matter of light.[1] Take away all light and the violet is black ; put it in a blaze of intensive light and it is scarcely visible. Between the two extremes of light lie every possible variation of the colour of the violet. It is a matter of vibrations, even of wireless waves, which can, indeed, produce colour as well as sound. The violet is no longer purple—it is not just pink or just blue—it contains more colours than the scientist can pick out.

What an exact mental analysis—yet often instantaneous—is needed for the artist to sense the colour of this violet under given conditions of light, and to record it in terms of fixed pigment ! After many experiments and much research he evolves his formula, which no other artist can exactly copy, for an artist's colouring is more individual than science allows ; it depends upon

[1] Noted by Bacon and carried further by Faraday.

touch, it depends upon feeling, even upon environment.

When the artist starts to record his reaction to the violet upon canvas, or even to record it, he is met by the necessity for a new analysis, and here he is greatly helped by his previous researches into the compoundings of colour. He knows which pigments to mix and which not to mix; he knows which to lay on first, and upon which ground to lay them; he knows what colours to glaze over his first colours to produce the result he wants. This was, virtually, settled for him before the end of the fourteenth century. But his own experience and experiment comes in when he finds by placing the violet against any other colour that the blue changes. Light plays its part all the time, but even when he has settled on his lighting, he is met by the almost intangible problem of the value of one colour against another. This is the science of colour values, well known to Cennino Cennini,[1] yet greatly developed by Turner, by Monet, by Gauguin— who by their analysis, by their experiments, have so completely revolutionized the use of colour in painting. This revolution came, naturally, along with the scientific development of the nineteenth century.[2] And it is in

[1] See *The Book of the Art of Cennino Cennini* (approx. 1398) translated by Christiana J. Herringham (George Allen and Unwin).
[2] See Chapter on Faraday.

this field of experiment and research that
Roerich stands pre-eminent, a pioneer who
has carried the science and practice of colour-
values further than his predecessors, and further
than it has been carried by any living artist.
The blinding blaze of colour in his exhibition
is due to his widening of the colour field.
In his works the colour is such that no printer
can attempt to reproduce it ; he uses the same
pigments as are sold in every shop, but with
them he achieves combinations which vibrate
to the eye in a new way. And this he has done
without crudity ; his colour-composition is
well blended, often soft and delicate—always
vibrating. And this immense effort, this addition to art, has been necessary to him simply
to express what he has *felt* in the things seen
or in the things imagined. He *felt* and he saw
more colour than was to be found in other
paintings ; his emotion and his intellect urged
him on till he could produce this extra-colour-
ing. Whether the use of pigment can ever
be pushed further, I doubt. The Roerich of
the future may play with wireless colour -
vibrations to get still more brilliant results.
When this occurs, Art and Science will again
be practised by one man !

This, however, is but a side of the technique
of a painter. There is also the question of
design. Drawing, however perfect, is elemen-
tary, even dull, until the soul of the artist

works out in personal touch and in original
design : and design, as all can see, is akin to
mathematics. A design can be copied, there
it differs from personal colouring. Yet the
mystery of a picture often lies as much in its
composition as in its colour.

The designs of Roerich are based upon memories of his archæological studies. But he has
used old forms only to give to them new life.
In design he is purely Russian ; yet he trans-
cends other Russians, so long as his imagination plays upon dreams evoked by Russia.
He has carried Russian art forward, yet after
his contact with Tagore, he *felt* Indian ; and
his Indian paintings, done in London, before
ever he visited India, were entirely Indian in
design as in conception. So original that
nothing like them had been done before, so
Indian that Tagore was amazed. It was in
London that Tagore and Roerich met and
became such intimate friends and understood
one another without words, for Tagore spoke
only his own language and English, while
Roerich spoke only Russian and French !

What they had in common was a unity of
Thought, a mutually accordant mysticism.

Where the scientific-mystic must restrain
his religious feelings and inspirations and only
dares to speak of what he can capture and
bring to earth by exact proof, the artist-mystic
may allow his spirit to soar ; he may speculate

on the Supernatural, and even seek to embody
it, without exact proof, in his work. He may
even portray what no eye has seen. This
Roerich has done : and because it is permissible
to an artist thus to capture the un-proved
emanations for which no material or physical
reason can be given, he is, in this, a freer man
than the scientist. With the same imple-
ments as any other artist, he can visualize and
record the unseeable. Perhaps, here, we light
upon the secret which makes a man of intellect
turn to Art ; binding him as it does by its own
stern disciplines of technique, it yet allows
him great freedom. In this direction, too,
Roerich has gone further than his immediate
predecessors and further than any of his contemporaries.

But this is at bottom a child-instinct, younger
than that of the meddlesome boy : and so it is
only natural that the history of art is longer
than the history of science, and that art was
fully developed when science was in its infancy.

Yet it is certain that in these days, many
men of genius who in earlier times would have
been artists—speculating scientifically in their
leisure moments—turn away from art in early
youth to devote themselves to science.

Science, on the whole, attracts the finest
minds to-day ; and it seems, as a rule, the
lesser brains, the less venturesome spirits,
the frailer physique (even the more effeminate)

which turn to Art. Nicholas Roerich is an exception to this rule, and in one sense he is a scientist, for he is notable in archæology. His collection of Russian archæological specimens was famous, and has influenced his imagination.

He is strong and tall, a vigorous and masculine man ; he is reserved, showing little of himself and, in his sphinx-like expression, one sees he is a mystic.

Yet he is a practical pioneer. His work and teaching at the Moscow Art Theatre, his designs for the " Sacre du printemps " (Stravinsky) preceded and influenced, if they did not actually dominate, much of the modern movement in the art of the present-day world, where no-one has yet been able to produce the dazzling colour which flows from him, let alone cover the vast range of imagination in design which his work embodies.

In quantity, too, he is positively giant-like. Over 600 of his paintings are collected at the Roerich Museum in America : and these are but a fraction of his output, which exceeds fifteen hundred. Each picture is in the nature of an experiment, but it is also a finished thing in itself : in this sense the artist is both experimenter and manufacturer. To acquire the technique of a Roerich, research must be added to the artist's pursuits, encompassing an analysis of nature comparable only to that of science.

In addition he must know all that can be known of the Chemistry of Colour (a subject which fascinated Davy for a time, causing him to work on the pigments of the ancients). Whoever has read Cennino Cennini[1] can no longer ignore the science that lies behind mastery of the technique of painting. It is because he has mastered this in theory and in practice that Roerich is a " Master." And his scientific instinct, which desires to improve upon what is known, has caused him to enlarge the whole scope of modern painting.

Yet he passed through London almost unnoticed—despite a large exhibition at the Goupil Gallery.

People entering this gallery were almost blinded by his colouring; and the mystic energy in his imaginative conceptions bewildered their mentality.

Like Bose, he covered a vast field—of united specializing—and as we let Bose go unnoticed for twenty years so have we let Roerich go, perhaps never to return.

A few in America appreciated, witness the museum which bears his name: but the United States could not hold him. Outcast from Russia, being non-Bolshevik, this giant took India and China in his stride, but it is Tibet that has proved to be his spiritual home. " Finished " in Russia, " finished " in London,

[1] *The Book of the Art of Cennino Cenneni.*

"finished" too in America, his vision yet carried him on, no longer young in body, but ever young in imagination. He went to the Himalayas and returned to New York with "such a collection of paintings as perhaps no one man has produced before."[1]

He journeyed to Tibet in search of the Spirit of Truth as it appears to him. And since then we have only silence. Few, even of his friends, seem to know if he is still alive.

As Bose proved the sciences of physics and biology and even psychology to be at One in Life, so has Roerich battled to pull the specific arts together. And after many vain attempts here and elsewhere, when the Russian cataclysm crushed his Moscow Organization, he at length established in New York his Master-School of all the Arts, to which, doubtless, he will return.

THE MAN

Impregnable as the rock and almost as silent, mysterious as the forest, is Nicholas Roerich, with his deep-set, small eyes, his egg-shaped head, and white face, his soft quiet voice, his big figure and workman-like hands. A man of few words, and with an indefinable atmosphere of meditation—like a monk; yet with him a

[1] A. C. Bossom (U.S.A.).

brilliant and devoted wife and several grown
children. To look at, more an intellectual
than an emotional type. Yet he might, in
other garments, pass for a Russian high-priest.

Evidently a man given up to solitary meditation, requiring little intercourse with his
fellow man—and a terrific worker.

What his trained eye perceives, orchestrates
itself anew in his brain, and is intensified in
his mind's eye ; and his artistic expression is
as though electrified, by the emotion condensed
in the Leyden jar of his vision. With a less
powerful imagination, he might have been
either just a distinguished archæologist, or else
a fashionable portrait painter.

What, then, is the source of the power,
working like a dynamo generating energy,
within him ?

First, visualise him in early days in his far
northern Russia, behind him centuries of
Norse ancestors, his appearance showing their
inherited characteristics. In such a place, his
Work naturally turned to digging for the lost
treasures of antiquity.; his love of Place sent
him enquiring into its history and hunting not
only for the wild animals of his forests, but for
the relics of the handicraft of his Folk. A
primitive hunter turned historian. The feelings thus aroused and the experiences thus
gained he would turn over in his mind and,
being religious by nature and tradition, he

would convert these, by the process of sublimation, in the white heat of ecstasy, into
Emotions, Ideas (Dreams) and Imagery. He
follows the bent of Imaged-Emotions and turns
these, by his handicraft, into Emotioned-
Imagery. But had his thought-process
stopped here he would have been a maker of
symbols—a traditional Ikon-maker. Just as
Bose might have been, at the same point, an
ordinary inventor, or Geddes an ordinary
architect, Branford a successful financier en-
dowing Art Galleries or causing Churches to
be built, or Weizmann an ordinary worker in
chemistry allowing his discoveries to be
commercialized. Just so Davy might have
been wood-carver in a cathedral, or Faraday
iron-worker to a Duke.

But in all these men there was that rare and
unaccountable element—imagery rising to
poetry, poetry rising to synthetic vision. All
these men are Seers, seeking to enlighten the
world.

Too many artists, even good ones, have
become Thought-Derelicts—or else at best
but worshippers of phantoms, when not of
fossils, and thus without guidance from religion
or ideal—old or new. But in Roerich there is
no such vague lack of purpose. He draws
upon his chord of Inner Life, and rhythm is of
its essence.

His art then is essentially a modern develop-

1 *The Interpreter.*

124

ment of the ancient folk-art of his own people, for which he has had a transforming enthusiasm—like the transforming force in his individual life history.

If all art, all science, all thought, all deed, is born of sublimation of the sex instinct,[1] then the force which produced a Roerich is explained.

But, as throughout this book, here again I suggest that physical organic force is not the whole of any greatly poetic personality, though it may well be the driving force which causes a Balzac to create two thousand characters, or a Roerich to, before he is sixty, complete over fifteen hundred large works.

But, one set of organs cannot account for all there is in any one of these works !

There is a Love which sets men on to the high and hard paths of great endeavour—making of them Divine Adventurers—a love which escapes the scope of science, and which therefore escapes its first analysis. Just as in the greater love, rarely seen it is true, between man and woman, a Divine Essence creeps in. There is, in short, an Ecstasy which escapes from the sex-impulse completely—and then only is real freedom discovered.

In short and unforeseen moments this freedom comes to men (and women) of genius—moments when all previous effort and thought

[1] The Interpreter.

suddenly kaleidoscopes into a single vision—
these are the moments of inspiration. And it
is this kind of inspiration which moves fine
minds to vast endeavours ; this is the vision
that drives them on over all obstacles, even to
victory over themselves, even at the cost of
suffering to others !

And it is this which one senses behind the
mountain of reserve observed in Nicholas
Roerich—an enormous and spiritual reserve-
force.

I am well aware that for some this may be
explained in one word as—Illusion. But this
needs explanation too !

We can leave it at this : there are forces in
the character of genius as yet not elucidated
by Science, and only dimly sensed by religion.

One scientific fact emerges : nature has
always produced (very few at a time) such
people—just as on the other extreme she
has continually produced types which, as
Leonardo da Vinci says, might as well be
nothing but a sack, tied in the middle, with
two openings, one to take in food and one to
emit it.

The mysteries of nature are not all solved :
and it is to the picturing of such mysteries
that Roerich devotes himself.

That there is in the artist and scientist alike
a passion for nature and truth is clear : in the
real artist to it is added a passionate love of

beauty—though each one has his own interpretation of this.

Listen, while this artist speaks :—

" Much discrimination must be projected,
not for the destruction but for the purification
of truth. Often it is the legend which is con-
firmed by facts. . . .

" Now at the moment of the revaluation of
our old standards we must take up fearlessly,"
he tells Americans, " the revision of our official
scientific sources. . . . Prejudice, one of our
most dangerous enemies in life, must be
destroyed with all the power of the Spirit ;
and only then quite easily the fragments of
truth can be woven together into a new and
wonderful texture, and this carpet shall help
us to fly from the real past to the real future,
and we shall discern that even the legendary
flying carpets no longer belong to fairy tales
but to life. Verily, a wonder-tale of all life
can be easily manifested to our average human
brain if it be directed without prejudice. Yet
not only in workmanship but even in beauty
we are sowing prejudice by going to the limits
of specialization. A strange aspect indeed is
this in art, when the painter can remain ignorant of music and the musician be silent before
a statue."[1]

Is this not the music of Bose over again—
played on a different instrument ?—especially

[1] Address by Nicholas Roerich.

as it comes after the artist's foundation of the Master Institute of United Arts in New York so strikingly corresponding to the Bose Institute of Sciences in Calcutta—and even across the continents within a few years one of the other !

Geddes would attempt to bring these two Institutes together and thus achieve his orchestration of the Arts and Sciences. And this, too, will come, though neither he nor Bose nor Roerich may be able at this date to arrive at it. *There is, in the world, a tremendous unseen force working slowly towards unity.*

Yet when in New York Roerich pronounced the unifying words about the Arts, he was confronted by shock and surprise that any connection should exist between the different branches of Art. The same shock and surprise with which Geddes and Bose have been met— the same determination to overcome it.

Roerich contends that this unity of the arts is not only an ideal matter, but of use in daily life. " Every sincere artist and every sincere scientist," he says, " can give you evidence as to this. And this searching of truth against conventionalism, against hypocrisy, must be the watchword of our days, for already we see a real, new generation arising, ready not only for struggle but for victory, crying, " Only Truth ! " " Only results ! " . . . " The position of art," he continues, " must be discussed

128

and reclassified. The place of art has been frequently misunderstood. . . . In Beauty only are diverse spirits united. The strings of Earth reach Heaven," he concludes, " only in the rhythms of Beauty."

Still under sixty, Nicholas Roerich was born in what we have now to call Leningrad. While yet a youth he exhibited, and was immediately recognized—a painting being purchased for the Tretliakoff Galleries—and success followed success until the Bolshevik revolution, which undermined his work, deprived him of his position and savings, and took his collections from him. He was now " finished," so far as his Russian career was concerned.

He came to London, where he worked with Dr. Young on the medical values of certain colours in the cure of various diseases.

Not only is he a man inspired, but he is an inspiration to others. Like Geddes, he is a World-Teacher, and by his distinguished educational efforts he has sown his seed in twenty different countries! His works shed their brilliance in The Louvre, The Luxemburg, and The Museums of London, Vienna, Prague, Venice, Milan, Brussels, Stockholm, Copenhagen and New York, Chicago, San Francisco, Detroit, as well as in private collections in most civilized lands.

Criticizing the current classifications, he asks, " Why separate Technology from Art and from

Science ? Why is sociology separated from politics, and why are these placed before religion ? "

Is it any wonder that he is, pre-eminently, a painter of ideas ?

Asked once about his " heroic and marvellous " Colour-schemes, he answered : " I use musical arrangements of colour, and this I can teach, but not by words." And then he added : " I want to express that while Nature is the creator, still the spectator of creation may also be a creator."

One day when I was marvelling at the deep knowledge his work displays of the linear facts of nature, cloud-forms, water, shapes and character of various trees, he said, " Realism has mystery, and mystery is very exact."

This seeing of exactness in mystery and of mystery in actual fact is as the typical of him as when he suddenly told me : " You know, I am a strong medium " ; and so let out the secret that he has done remarkable drawings with his eyes closed when experimenting with spiritualism !

These drawings he calls " unconscious expressions "—when doing them his pencil often travels over the same lines like the pencil of a blind man. It was while experimenting with table-turning that he knew, " unconsciously," that Tagore would come to London—two months before the poet actually arrived.

Spiritualism interests him as a mysterious
nature-force about which nothing is known.

Now, although deeply versed in Folk-lore
and being in a very real sense a Folk-artist
first of all, another fact about him is that he is
inventing a new Lore, for he paints Sagas
of his own imagining, and in this is a maker of
modern symbols.

For example, one picture suggests that there
is not enough anger in Heaven, and so when
they want some they send an angel who puts
his sword into earthly passions and takes the
heat of the earth back to Heaven, whose
inhabitants, for want of this might atrophy.
This is merely a humorous picture—but how
lovely !

Another side of his character came out when
he suddenly stood before a picture, and said to
me, " Who can solve the problem of construction of a mighty waterfall ? Yet in its foam
and scum lies hidden a great creative outline."

As a painter he cannot be summed up—
some say he is mystical, others that he is
decorative, others that he is a symbolist,
others that he is archaic, while others again
see him as a great nature-student, as a realist—
and he is really all these things—and more :
he escapes the pigeon-holes, and, like Geddes,
is in them all, and in new ones of his own
making.

Is there any point in asking where he

studied ? The whole world is his studio. His
position in Russian art before the revolution
was that of a leader among pioneers, and
wherever he goes to live he soon has a similar
position.

Very literally, indeed, did Andreyev speak
of " Roerich's Kingdom " in the last essay he
ever wrote—devoted to a study of this artist!
" Roerich," he said, " is not a servant of the
earth . . . he is all in his own world . . .
here it is as though the wondrous world of
Roerich and the old familiar earth converged,
and this is so because all those for whom the
free sea of dreams and contemplation has
opened, well-nigh inevitably land at Roerich's
shores, which " are not of these parts."

And that this is so, Andreyev thought, is
largely because Roerich " is of the North."—
in whose long nights dreams come to men with
strange vitality—reaching " the borderland
of clairvoyance "—for this artist is one who
" amidst the visible discovers the unseen ",[1]
not by instruments, however magic, by means
of which science performs this same feat, but by
ordinary means.

" There. is nothing alarming ", this artist
said to me, " in the contrast between the
beauty of the town and the beauty of nature.
Just in the same way as fine contrasting colours
do not kill each other but form a new powerful

[1] Andreyev.

chord, so the beauty of the town and the beauty of nature dwell hand in hand, intensifying each other. They are the two tones of the chord—its third tone being the beauty of the unknown ".

Here is a hint of that philosophy which is ever present in all his work and life—for he, like our scientists, is naturally a philosopher. And this is why, from a youthful illustrator of ancient Russia, he has developed into a seer.

" Building up a new spiritual attitude in his own sphere, Roerich is taking part in re-shaping our inner life as a whole " :[1]   he is " certainly one with the life after death, with nature and our earth. *This oneness is organic with him* ".[2]

" In our day ", he says himself, " there is an undoubted return to savagery of an enormous number of people, and only beauty and wisdom can bring back to humanity all the easiness of the spirit it has lost. Upon art and science is founded that true impulse of construction which will illuminate all future achievements of humanity." In this belief he gives time freely and energy to spare—quietly as is his nature, for the side of pioneer social reform in which his faith leads him.

In London he cries : " In the name of Knowledge and Beauty let us combine for struggle and work ; we do not feel hunger or starvation ;

[1] Baltrushitis.   [2] Zarintzev.

we do not shiver because of the cold. We tremble because of the vacillation of our spirit."

Hearing of a family which because of deprivation, in despair put an end to themselves, Roerich said, " Now that is intolerably faint-hearted."

He sees the wings of new knowledge and of new beauty already growing : he says, " We are not alone in our struggle ! "

And this is the son of a barrister !

But of a barrister who brought up his son chiefly in the country, on a great estate of ten thousand acres with endless primeval forest, great lakes and those very mounds in which the artist as a youth hunted for real " buried treasure " and discovered the actual bones of the Vikings of old from whom he is descended.

PART II

THE DEAD : BY WHOSE LIGHT WE LIVE

Mr. Frauncis Bacon of " Tribute or giving what is dew " :
   " The praise of the worthiest virtue
   The praise of the worthiest affection.
   The praise of the worthiest power.
   The praise of the worthiest person ".[1]

[1] From *A Conference of Pleasure* (edited by James Spedding, 1870).

" For the commandment is a lamp and the law is light."

Proverbs vi, 23.

CHAPTER I

Bacon[1]

" I thought myself born to be of advantage to mankind
. . . I have taken all knowledge to be my province ".
F. B.

" He is the father of experimental philosophy."
Voltaire.

SOMETIMES there comes into the world a man of
noble birth whose nature rather than his circumstances compels him to enter into intellectual struggles and immense labours.

Occupation for mind and body he has in
plenty—Court duties, and duties to the State.
The days of such a man are filled with respon-
sibilities, and hence with occupations enough
to fill the life of any man.

But occasionally there arises one, like
Balfour, for instance, for whom even all this
life, between Court and country, is not enough.
Balfour, even while playing in addition a lead-

[1] " The re-organisation of the sciences and the exposition
of a new method by which the human mind might proceed
with security and certainty toward the true end of all human
thought and action ; also the digesting and codifying of the
chaotic mass of English Law " (*Encycl. Britt.*).

ing part in the conducting of the Great War, found time hang on his hands and so published, in the heat of warfare, his *Humanism versus Theism !* Presumably merely to satisfy his inner craving for projecting his mind towards the Infinite—a sort of prayer.

A painter told me once that every picture should be a prayer of thanksgiving for natural beauty.

Only if we look at this need in man for the moral equivalent of Prayer, can we understand the immense labours undertaken, apart from any need of what the world could give, by a man like Bacon ; and it is perhaps the answer to all the questions I have left unanswered in this study of various men of genius, each of whom might say, " My work is my prayer."

Research may then be summed up as an act of worship, and discovery as a prayer answered ?

Psycho-analysts may ask what is meant by prayer, and what the cause of the act of worship.

It is evident that there is in man a need (as is seen, for example, in Bach with his twenty children) beyond even that of procreation, to project himself beyond everyday humanity, to attune himself to something outside his senses, outside the world as he knows it, and to bring new order where at first he only sees perplexity. This he may achieve in a scientific or a philosophical way, in a religious way, or in an artistic way.

Whichever he chooses, he rises on the wings of imagination—he moves in the world of Dreams.

The noble, with every material desire satisfied, with every chance to satisfy the sexual urge in many ways, when he turns to its sublimation can only be said to do so to save his soul—(to use the antique phrase). And this is, perhaps, the prime cause for the life-work of every pioneer in science and in art, though not at present reducible to strictly scientific terms.

There is in it, possibly, some process of the self-intoxication known to all mystics ; there must be some dynamic force at work which psycho-analysis has not yet elucidated, a force only found—and still too rarely—in human beings.

Up to a point Bacon compares with Balfour —his public work is political and legal ; he takes his part as a leader in the making of English History ; and his hobby is philosophy.

But his nature carries him beyond ordinary contemplative study : he creates, like Geddes, a new system of thought, he gives some fresh direction to human ideas. He is a Pathfinder, a hewer of intellectual roads, an adventurer of the spirit, blazing a fresh trail, trampling over the undergrowths of more than two thousand years.

Mentally he is an explorer. He explores the Infinite, yet to definite purpose.[1]

Bacon was a man who did not hesitate to receive " graft " in public life ; and who yet, in his inmost self, burned to serve mankind.

He was a paradox ; and in money matters, paradoxically enough, he had none of the scruples of the subjects of my other portraits.

The inner self in Bacon's case seems to have been inherited—for his mother was a Puritan, burning with religious zeal. His moral slackness in public life did not come from his father, who was, in his son's words, " plain, direct and constant ". It might be traced to some other forbear, or to the environment of Court life—or perhaps he was merely a spoilt child—as the youngest of a large family ?

His early delicate health may account for his habit of contemplation, for he never took part in games or sports as a boy ; and he must have started while still young the solitary walks which led to much thinking. Indoors the boy interested himself in conjuring, or sleight-of-hand, at which he became very ingenious.

And, while still a boy, he appeared at Court so thoughtful that the Queen, herself in love with learning, picked him out and called him her young Lord Keeper. Fascinated, he might

[1] " The restoration to man of that command over Nature which he had lost by the Fall " (*Encycl. Britt.*).

well have vowed himself at a very early age, to serve the Queen.

At thirteen, he is already at Cambridge, where Whitgift, the Master of his College (Trinity) was a future Archbishop of Canterbury—and, who, note, " seems to have been an unprincipled Divine ".[1]

Learning in those days was devoted to Aristotle ; and even in early youth, Francis Bacon seems to have rebelled against this : it did not satisfy him—and this revolt is the root of all his future thinking. The learning of his day was too narrow for him, even as the specialisms of our day have been too tight for Geddes, Bose, Branford and Roerich.

Bacon, too, delicate in health though he was, began as a boy itching to throw over the traces —to widen the horizon—perhaps at first with a little of the instinct that urges other boys to break records—maybe behind his revolt at first there lay, inhibited and dormant, the sporting instinct to out-distance his fellows.

But why, in an age still governed by Aristotle from his grave, did this solitary youth find him unsatisfactory ? Left hungry by the mental food available, in his early teens, he forms the by no means humble notion that he will bring about a complete revolution in knowledge !

Like a gazelle feeding on barren ground, Hunger prompts him to seek food elsewhere.

[1] *Francis Bacon,* by Israel Levine (Leonard Parsons).

The mental environment of his time plays a large part in the development of his creative energy. In a sense he is as bold a colonizer as Sir Walter Raleigh; and the same age of adventure nourished them both.

The fire burns more brightly in a frost, as though roused to bigger effort by the need for harder struggle.

Hunger of the spirit (define it how you will) is a creative urge. But for it the "Novum Organum" might never have been conceived; but for it there would have been no saints or martyrs.

Bacon, however, was in public life anything but saintly. In fact he was something of a time-server, and even of a blackguard!

On the one hand as a boy he had the diverse influences of a Puritan mother and of an unscrupulous Archbishop—on the other a field of study that left him hungry and dissatisfied.

Torn between these influences, this mixed environment, he courageously pioneered for himself along the path where he thought Truth might be discovered—for he had within him a passion for the Truth, in spite of, or because of, the hypocrisy of the Court life in which he grew up. And this notion of his own gradually became his predominating passion.

His struggle was towards the growth of his own soul. It was his only " escape "—the only thing in which his life could not satisfy him.

BACON

Starting as a youthful " craze ", it developed into a quest—strengthened, no doubt, by the influences at work in France, filled as it was with political and religious strife, at the time of his stay there (1576), only four years after the massacre of St. Bartholomew ; it was just one year before Drake started his voyage round the world, and thirteen years before Galileo led the way to Faraday by founding—in the teeth of bitter opposition—-the science of dynamics !

A quarter of a century had still to pass before Shakespeare produced *Hamlet ;* but there was so great a stirring in Europe as Bacon grew to manhood, that it was but natural he should take his part in it. Hence though his *Novum Organum* was not published till 1620, yet it is the direct product of these early influences, this exciting environment.

In attempting the analysis of other characters in this volume I have had in mind the Charting of Life,[1] worked out in terms of Place, Work and Folk ; but much can also be worked out on the basis of Time, Energy and Space ; and this, did space allow, might better suit the philosophy of Bacon.

He was eminently the product of his time, which evolved a mental energy not repeated till our own day.

It seems as though, in the rhythm of history, such a period comes every few hundred years,

[1] *The Interpreter.*

and is preceded by Precursors and culminates in Pioneers, in every field of thought and action.

Such times are periods of great unrest and struggle, symbolical of germination, of Birth.

Yet none of his many brothers and sisters, few indeed of his friends, were moved by the impulses which moved Bacon to scale his lonely heights.

Imagine these eyeing him askance, even jeering at him, perhaps squabbling with him in private. Neither environment nor inheritance can exactly explain his genius.

Circumstance plays its part, too, in Bacon's career.

At the impressionable age of eighteen he is called from France to the death-bed of Sir Nicholas Bacon, his father, Elizabeth's Lord Keeper of the Privy Seal ; and he, the youngest of a large family, receives but a small portion of the inheritance. Enough, had he wished, to provide for a life only devoted to science and high thinking ; but, reared to high living, he must continue this too.

A St. Francis would have left the world and given himself up to the service of God ; but Bacon was no saint.

The life Bacon desired must now to a certain extent be earned ; he must adopt a profession.

He decides for the Law and settles in Gray's Inn. Hard work, admitting no other interests, ensues. Even his digestion suffers from it !

BACON

Pleasure is set aside in the pursuit of professional skill.

After years of this he gets himself elected to Parliament—for the Law is, to many, the stepping-stone to Politics, and especially in a youth whose uncle is the Queen's chief adviser. He is shrewd enough, worldly enough, to realize he has influence.

He writes to his uncle, and is rebuked for arrogance. The nephew replies tactfully, but firmly, repudiating arrogance " more than other vice," and says his natural bashfulness is often mistaken for pride.

His own description of himself may well be the true one—for it is common to sensitive and delicate persons. Though snubbed, he goes on quietly with his law studies and his politics, biding his time.

Eight years later he puts his pride in his pocket—which as a Courtier he had long learnt to do—and again he writes to his uncle :—

" I wax now somewhat ancient," he says ; and points out that he has always hoped to serve the Queen, not for personal glory or wealth, but because he considers her worthy of his service !

In this famous letter he assures his uncle of small worldly ambitions. " I have as vast contemplative ends as I have moderate civil ends," he writes ; " for I have taken all knowledge to be my province." Here he shows the

145

dream of boyhood has been carried over into
manhood (he is now 31); for he declares that
he desires to effect a radical change in knowledge, to establish a " new and real scientific
method which will result in profitable inventions and discoveries."

This last practical suggestion maturing
years have added to his dream—enhanced and
not lessened by his present struggle for the
ample and opulent life to which by birth he
felt his right.

He himself admits this desire may be the urge
of " curiosity or vain-glory, or nature, or
(if one take it favourably) *philanthropia* ; "
and he adds that it is so fixed in his mind that
it " cannot be removed."

But before he will devote himself to this aim
(by no means humble !) he must be established
financially, and politically, he thinks.

Here we have a type of man very different
from the others described in this book !

Had he failed to make for himself the position he desired in the world his *Philanthropia*
would have perhaps been buried !

This curious complexity in his character is
very unlike any other thinking man of his
magnitude. One can hardly imagine Socrates,
Leonardo, or Shakespeare putting good living
first—and from the age of twenty-three to
almost middle-life. It is as though he tried
to subdue his spirit to the conventions of his

station in life. The Hunger of his spirit must wait to be fed, his soul must wait to be freed, until he has made his body comfortable!

Was there some nobly born lady behind all this? Even so it is a weakness not to be seen in any other great philosopher.

At this moment—in the year following the well-known letter—his sense of political duty comes to the front, and he opposes a vote in Parliament which seeks to give the Queen an unusually large grant of money, which he thinks encroaches on the rights of the Commons to exercise control over supplies. Almost in the spirit of Hampden and Cromwell, this!

He is out-voted, and his stand costs him the Queen's favour.

Again his pride goes into his velvet pocket, and he writes to his uncle, trying to explain himself and hoping to be pardoned. But no; the Queen forbids him to Court. And this at a time when he has applied for the vacant post of Attorney-General!

His *Philanthropia* is giving him trouble after all! After years of silence it pops up its head at a most unfortunate moment!

The worldly Bacon is not to be lightly influenced or dismissed, however, even by his *alter ego ;* and now he makes the most of his intimacy with Essex, the Queen's favourite and a man of intellect—and to him he discloses his plan for his progress of humanity.

How the two sides of the dual nature work together in him at times ! Here he is actually *using* his *Philanthropia* to regain the position it had lost him !

Essex is won over ; but he cannot win the Queen. Coke is appointed—Bacon is passed over.

Coke's appointment left vacant the post of Solicitor General : Bacon, backed by Essex, applied for it—and was again passed over.

The philosopher is now an energetic place-seeker, pitting his obstinacy against that of the Queen.

Spending beyond his income, he refuses to be driven down the social hill. Money troubles and uncertainties tell on his delicate health.

Why did not such a great mind leave the world at this period, and take to the study as the cloister, for which his income was sufficient ?[1]

At this moment he was, in his chosen career, " un homo finito."[2]

He describes it as a time of " exquisite disgrace." His rivals accused him of unworthy cringing.

Imagine, then, the man who was to write the *Novum Organum* in the act of cringing for worldly position ! Did he despise himself at this period ?

[1] " And so give over all care of service and become some sorry bookmaker—or a true pioneer in that mine of truth." Francis Bacon (*Encycl. Britt.*).
[2] Papini.

Certainly it had its influence over his future worldly acts, and exercised a demoralizing influence on him. Certainly there was weakness in his character to which he, from time to time, gave way.

Essex, who is devoted to him, now insists on giving him an estate worth £1,800, and in return Bacon is content to influence the Queen anonymously and by proxy, giving without stint his service and advice to her favourite!

Essex and Bacon are almost one man; and when Essex falls into disfavour, Bacon exerts himself on his friend's behalf.

Now the Queen begins to grow milder towards her favourite's adviser; and she employs him, though unofficially, as one of her Learned Counsel.

All this time he is burying the spirit, and currying Court favour—like any other deposed courtier.

Essex, hot-headed and impetuous, having quarrelled with the Queen, suddenly undertakes some revenge and breaks out in rebellion. He is brought to trial. Coke and Bacon are in charge of the proceedings.

This man, whose *Philanthropia*, in his own words, " cannot be removed," now tries and condemns to execution his most intimate and zealous friend—rather than resign his own professional position which he owes to this same friend!

Popular feeling goes against the sentence, and to justify herself the Queen needs a public report to be made. Bacon is ordered to write it, and, says a biographer,[1] " he had no choice but to comply."

Of course he had a choice. Once again he could have retired to a life of pure contemplation! Now, it seems, spiritually, he is a completely " finished " man.

Is he not convicted in his own mind of the blackest treachery and ingratitude ?

In his speeches at the trial—not one word of friendship, pity, or emotion !

Can it be that he is deeply moved by a sense of public duty ? (for Essex had plotted foolishly against the Crown). Has he now put his feelings aside, as once before he put his well-being aside, from a clear impersonal sense of duty ?

We must remember that he is still in financial trouble, living beyond his means, and cannot afford to lose favour. Already he had once been arrested for debt, and by a goldsmith. Already he had thought of marrying a wealthy widow—who married his rival, Coke, instead.

Who can see, in all this, one of the giants of idealism ?

Was there ever such complexity ?

How analyse the character of such a man— rendered desperate and despicable by the struggle to keep his foothold in the world his intellect despised !

[1] Israel Levine.

The Queen he had sworn to serve for her own deserts alone (and not for peace or power or even for money) now dies (1603).

James succeeds, and to him Bacon immediately writes—and even to friends and acquaintances who may have influence, for he is a desperate man.

His cousin, Robert Cecil, has helped him in a financial crisis ; and to him he now writes, " As for my ambition . . . I do assure your honour mine is quenched " ; and yet he adds (complex as ever) " My ambition now I shall only put upon my pen, whereby I shall be able to maintain memory and merit of times succeeding."

Crushed ! Submissive ! Cringing !

Yet *Philanthropia* not quite dead, rises to add a word to save his pride.

And this is the man to whom some ascribe all the works of Shakespeare !

Well, a man who could stand so aloof, condemning his one friend to death and disgrace, might set aside his own worst nature while contemplating Divinity. In a very real sense did his *Philanthropia* save his soul ; it was his only possible escape from the results of his own weakness.

It is strange no one has ever suggested that Shakespeare may be the author of the *Novum Organum* ! But, of course, Bacon, who does not at present look the man to have done it, took care there should be no mistake about that.

And it is now that he does give a year or two to intellectual labours ; not forgetting to write of himself that he was born, he believes, " for the service of mankind—fitted for nothing so well as for a study of the Truth."

The plot deepens !

He declares his over-mastering passion to be the love of knowledge and he " hates every kind of imposture."

Re-action, of course, has set in. And he produces one of the two great works of his life.

Proficience and Advancement of Learning— being " a survey of the state of existing knowledge and penetrating criticism of current knowledge "—the very thing that has lain dormant in him since boyhood — and he is now nearly 45 !

This masterpiece of free thinking, he dedicates, characteristically, though according to custom, to the King, but with words of such fulsome praise that they can only be summed up as Hypocrisy !

Would Milton have curried favour by such means ? Could Milton have produced such a work ?

These questions run one into the other ! In Bacon the gold and the dross are united :

impossible to separate them. The two taken
together are—the man.

Having delivered his mind, he is soon back
again at his profession, this time advising the
King.

What is behind this overmastering worldliness in one of the truest philosophers the world
has known—in one who laid the foundations
of modern thought ?

Long before this age our other pioneers are
happily married ; in the life of Bacon so far
there seems no outstanding love-affair (unless,
for we must not flinch, with Essex, whom he
condemned to death ?). He is not famous for
gallantry, history tells of no intrigues. What
drives him on, against his " better self ? "

This is a mystery unsolved.

If ever a man was torn in two, he was ; yet
always the world triumphed.

Now he begins to win the success he struggled
for, and now, too, his conscience troubles him,
and he publishes (1604) *Apology in certain
imputations concerning the late Earl of Essex*,
perhaps as much to curry public favour as to
ease his own mind.

" I would not show myself false-hearted nor
faint-hearted for any man's sake living."

Public opinion is satisfied—his public career
is safe.

He is knighted. He marries Alice Barnham,
" an alderman's daughter, an handsome

maiden, to my liking " ; and even at his marriage he is as extravagant as ever, making
" his wench " buy large stores of gold and silver
clothing ; and a year later he wins the place
he once struggled for in vain ; he becomes
Solicitor-General—but he is still in debt !

And all this time his great work goes forward
—almost secretly.

When does he find a moment to spare for
it ?

Small wonder if its progress is slow.

How can he retain even a side of his mind
in sustained or concentrated meditation on a
subject which admits of no hiatus ?

For he now throws himself into the political
agitations of the hour, and leads in advising
the King on financial matters ; " for two
or three years he had a firm grip on the political
situation."[1] And he becomes (1613) Attorney-
General, and (1617) Lord Keeper of the Privy
Seal.

In all this he has to be obedient not only to
James I but to Buckingham.

How could so independent and great a
thinker so tune himself to petty submission ?

Once at least he permits himself to write,
and to Buckingham :—

" This matter of pomp, which is Heaven to
some men, is Hell to me, or Purgatory at
least."

[1] Israel Levine.

Yet had he not put himself there ?

Success on the Chart of Life,[1] is Comedy, and this the Greeks knew when they discerned its Muse, Thalia.[1]

And Bacon, who so hated mental restrictions, had imposed one upon himself the like of which no other man in history has been able so fully to maintain. He so disciplined his mind, his feelings, his imagination, that he kept a cloister undefiled within himself, fertile and creative to an amazing extent, separate from his public life.

He drew on the full chord of life for the achievement of his sublimated dream—yet never, or very seldom, did he allow it to penetrate his demoralized professional existence !

Surely never has there been another man to lead so intensely a double life !

And there seems the less excuse for it when we consider the high degree of intellect fashionable in the Courts of his day.

Had he chosen to live quietly on his income, working out his revolution in methods of thinking, he would none the less have achieved fame and power.

But on he went with his comedy, riding for a fall.

" It is said he was more the possessor of intellect than of heart,"[2] but he kept even his enormous intellect divided against himself !

[1] *The Interpreter.*   [2] Israel Levine.

155

He drove a rare tandem with extraordinary dexterity.

As Lord Chancellor he " laid down the duties of his office with great dignity and nobility."[1]

Yet now he allowed himself to be drawn into an intrigue—in which his old rival, Coke, was concerned. It is profitless to follow this here in detail. It was a matter of marrying Coke's daughter to Buckingham's brother, and Coke's wife was averse to the match. Eventually in the legal proceedings of the struggle, Bacon became involved. He did not foresee that the King would side with Coke—but as soon as this was obvious Bacon withdrew his own objections to the match, abjectly. He grovelled submissively to Buckingham at the same time.

Honours are showered on him, he becomes Lord Chancellor and is given the lease of York House ; in the same year he is created a Peer of the Realm.[2] And, two years later, as if to cheat the Devil, he publishes his *Novum Organum*, at the age of 59.

The next year he is made a Viscount ; tales of his tremendous extravagance run higher than ever !

In exchange for his titles he has to favour, in Chancery, suits brought by persons in favour with Buckingham or the King.

In a word he abuses justice, of which he

[1] Israel Levine.   [2] *Idem.*

is the chief keeper in the land, and quite submissively : he even *recommends* torture to
secure evidence against a prisoner. Thus, in
1619, with all his wisdom and experience, he
closes his eyes to possible consequences.
Politics are in an upheaved state, when suddenly a petition is presented to the House
accusing Bacon of having accepted a bribe
some years before.

He is alarmed, but he writes to Buckingham : " Your Lordship spake of Purgatory.
I am now in it, but my mind is calm."

The charges are proved, the corruption is a
fact. Bacon, his weakness showing publicly
for the first time, breaks down and is unable to
appear. He writes to Parliament asking time
to prepare his defence. But he makes his will
in preparation for the worst.

The enquiry starts and the Lord Chancellor
abandons hope, resigns his Seal—confesses !

Further charges are brought. He confesses
to them all—and pleads for mercy.

What could be more despicable ?

Within four months he fell from favour—
and was too weak to be present to hear his
sentence depriving him forever of all that he
had won—for which he had sold himself so
thoroughly ; and which sent him to the Tower
" during the King's pleasure ". A " finished "
man indeed. He is in fact a convicted
criminal.

But he soon secures release from the Tower —he has strength enough left for that.

He retires to his country estate and writes to Buckingham : " I thank God I have overcome the bitterness of this cup by Christian resolution, so that worldly matters are but mint and cummin ".

His boyhood's dream is steadfast, unbroken, it saves him.

Yet he is still anxious to be reinstated in the King's favour, still harassed by debts (in which he asks James to help him), and it looks as though his letter to Buckingham is the result of a passing mood.

His health gets worse—even his wife fails him. Yet through the whole of this he works out his dream : now in his *Natural History*, now in his *New Atlantis*, where he speaks of " means to convey sounds in strange lines and distances ", of powerful engines for rapid transport, of " some degree of flying in the air ", and of ships and boats for going under water : he translates his own *Advancement of Learning* into Latin that it may be more widely read by Scholars : he studies the causes of colour and fixes the means whereby Newton afterwards found out the composition of Light : he describes the Laws of Attraction[1] : and he adds to his Essays.

[1] " Mais ce qui m'a le plus surpris ç'a été de voir dans son livre en termes exprès, cette attraction dont M. Newton passe pour l'inventeur."—*Voltaire*.

BACON

When he is sixty-five, and driving in a heavy snowfall, he stops his coach because the snowfall has suggested to him an experiment in refrigeration, and he wishes to see if snow will preserve flesh from putrefaction. He buys a chicken, stuffs it with snow. Chill and bronchitis result of thus exposing himself.

"The experiment," he writes, "is successful"; but in consequence of it he dies.

What an unfathomable life!

Was he a hypocrite?

How could he lead his life of noble contemplation in the midst of such a life of strenuous but ignoble action?

Can any machine stand such constant and sudden readjustments as his mind must have made every day of his grown-up life?

Where did it acquire its extraordinary suppleness—perhaps suggested when as a little boy he made himself expert in conjuring tricks?

Was everything to him merely a game? Science and philosophy a game to play at home; law and politics a game to play in public— and in each to gain mastery as the record-breaker?

In the home game his desire is to be a saviour of mankind, in the public game to govern the State. Was he a megalo-maniac?—this man who, as Levine puts it, desired " to be (and was) a pioneer in a new movement of human progress "?

A megalo-maniac achieves nothing. Bacon transcended the Comedy of Success and the Epic of Career.

His home game was real, though the other went up in smoke. This endures.

He changed the outlook in scientific knowledge, and thus foresaw and aided the radical transformation of the whole outward circumstances of human life.

In him, to use old words, God and the Devil seem to have kept an even balance, and each in a degree of strength seldom found in one man. Each one of us is conscious of this dual nature in ourselves, but, torn as we may be at times, we do not scale the heights in both directions at once, as did Bacon—whose vision was greater even than his science, great as that was ; and whose spirit penetrates all serious literature and all serious science to this day.

His character almost defies analysis. He was a thorough and a despicable scoundrel ; and yet, at the same time, he was a great lawyer, a fascinating personality, and *" a man so rare in knowledge of so many several kinds, endowed with the facility and felicity of expressing it all in so elegant, significant, so abundant and yet so choice and ravishing a way of words, of metaphors, of allusions—as perhaps the world has not seen since it was a world."*[1]
But he had no sense of humour.[2]

[1] Sir Tobias Matthews (1660).
[2] Though he said of himself that he " rang the bell which called the wits together." (*Encycl. Britt.*).

CHAPTER II

DAVY

" Life we term a spark, a fire, a flame :
And then we call that fire, that flame, immortal,
Although the nature of all fiery things
Belonging to the earth is perishable.

. . . .

And that which kindleth the whole frame of nature
Has no abiding place, although its source is ever-
lasting".

H. DAVY.

In Penzance (1778) there lived, " shiftless, thriftless," a wood-carver " of lax habits," whose son became famous at school because of his gifts for story-telling and for composing poetry.[1] As he grew up this boy played truant to go off fishing. And while standing dreaming by the flowing river bank there developed in his mind a quest. In love with Nature, he told himself stories, and words ran rythmically in his head ; his quest was his poem.

Was it by chance that Humphrey Davy

---

[1] T. E. Thorpe, F.R.S. (*Humphrey Davy*, Cassell and Co.) said :—" Davy's abilities were not perceived by his masters (but were) fully recognized by his schoolfellows."

came into the world only eight years after Wordsworth ?

With his father he learnt to use his hands, but he decided a wood-carver he would never be ! He'd rather be a fisherman or an adventurer—but casting about for a way to embark on his quest, to express his passion, he found the field hedged in ; life in Penzance did not offer much opportunity.

At length, after much meandering (which in a healthy boy means much thinking, and trying things out) he got himself apprenticed to a Surgeon. Having practised on wood and then on fishes, he thought he might develop skill in carving disease out of human bodies.[1]

In spite of the nature of his chosen calling, he still wrote verses, read poetry, and at the same time turned to chemistry in his leisure hours. Not satisfied with mere school while at School—not satisfied with mere surgery while at Surgery ! The quest, unfulfilled, made him restless. And so he left the Pen-

[1] At this time (1795) in one of his earliest notebooks he wrote down the subjects he set himself to study :—I. *Theology* or Religion (taught by Nature), and ethics or moral virtues (by Revelation). II. *Geography*. III. *My Profession*—1, Botany ; 2, Pharmacy ; 3, Nosology ; 4, Anatomy ; 5, Surgery ; 6, Chemistry. IV. *Logic*. V. *Languages*—1, English ; 2, French ; 3, Latin ; 4, Greek ; 5, Italian ; 6, Spanish ; 7, Hebrew. VI. *Physics*—1, The doctrines and properties of natural bodies ; 2, of the operations of Nature ; 3, of the doctrines of fluids ; 4, of the properties of organised matter ; 5, of the organisation of matter ; 6, simple astronomy ; 7, mechanics ; 8, rhetoric and oratory ; 9, history and chronology ; 10, mathematics.

162

zance Surgeon and moved on : on to Clifton,
where his vision developed as he worked at
chemistry—and his passion found outlet in
poetry, which brought him into friendship
with Coleridge and Southey.

And here it was that he started on his quest,
experimenting with gases and, like every
Knight of the Grail, he more than once nearly
lost his life.

Here this poet discovered laughing-gas.

His quest now began to develop into a mission. He was offered and accepted an appointment as lecturer at the Royal Institution in
London (1801); and it was there that Fate
brought thirteen years later, to this son of a
wood-carver that son of a blacksmith who was
to open the way into our modern electrical
civilization.

" O, Thou! whose fancies from afar are brought :

* * *

*May rather seem to brood on air than on an earthly
   stream "*.[1]

It is significant—since indeed of the very
nature of the industrial revolution in which
skill and science, invention and discovery,
have gone on together—that these sons of the
wood-carver and of the blacksmith owed so
much to the son of a hand-loom weaver ; for
the corner-stone of their work was laid by one

[1] Wordsworth.

John Dalton, who first " enunciated the Atomic Theory which explained the fundamental laws of chemical combination,"[1] and opened the way to the new experiments with electro-chemistry which Davy and Faraday were to elaborate with such world-shaking results.

Dalton was born only twelve years before Davy ; and so this man went on his Mission environed by such world-movers as Dalton and Faraday, such poets of nature as Words-worth, Coleridge and Southey.

Angling — Poetry — Medicine — what are these doing together in the unsatisfied heart of one truant youth, and contending to drive him on from wood-carving and story-telling to chemistry and philosophy? What of his inner struggle to reduce these three to one ?

There seems to live in such men a clearly-defined urge towards Unity. There was poetry in his chemistry, there was science in his philo-sophy. In all he did there was the eager, seeking patience of the angler, the light hand of the skilled carver ; and research to him was a development of story-telling. In him as in Dalton and Faraday, you see the modern development of the ancient handicraftsman.

The Royal Institution, where he henceforth lived and worked, is still standing, very little altered in appearance. What a marvellous story it would make for him could he step into

[1] *History of Chemistry*, by Sir E. Thorpe, F.R.S.

his old laboratory and see how it has been transformed—see the experiments going on there to-day—the consummation of his dreams !

Could his soul have contained the poetry that would have surged in him had he seen young Jagadis Bose experimenting there less than a century later ?—experimenting in the Davy-Faraday Laboratory where his name and that of his assistant are forever kept alive, where work is done which, but for them, might never have been started?

Cool and classical it stands, one of the landmarks of eighteenth century London—The Royal Institution of Great Britain—workplace, even home, of many pioneers.

The missionaries of science still lecture in his small auditorium—surely one of the most impressive lecture-halls in the world, to enter which provides a thrill aroused and accentuated by the wonders there so long, and still, given utterance.

Called back from medicine to agriculture, by some thought-process due to memories of his old environment, to seeds sown during his truant days, Davy's fame rose to its height through his researches in agricultural chemistry. On this subject he delivered epoch-making lectures to brilliant audiences attracted by his poetic eloquence and the newness of his discoveries.

Six years before his meeting with Faraday,

however, he was already on the path of electricity, and followed it up till he made the grand discovery that the alkalies and the earths are compound substances formed by oxygen *united* with metallic bases. He discovered a new metal, potassium—was the first to use electrolysis—and his delight was ecstatic!

Here was poetry indeed!

Then he discovered five other new metals : sodium, barium, strontium, calcium and magnesium.

What fun! Mentally and practically angling for new metals!

And he proved the earths to consist of metals *united* to oxygen. Always this seeking for unity!

About this time, and three days after he had been knighted, he married[1] a lady of wealth—curiously unromantic his marriage[2]—and so in 1813 he resigned his Chair at the R.I., and, having a new theory of volcanic action now ready to be put to the test—his truant spirit freed from harness—he went off to the Con-

[1] (a) Davy wrote to his mother : " I believe I should never have married but for this charming woman, whose views and whose tastes coincide with my own, and who is eminently qualified to promote my best efforts and objects in life ".

(b) Sir Joseph Banks, P.R.S., wrote : " Davy, our secretary, is on the point of marrying a rich and handsome widow, who has fallen in love with science and marries him in order to obtain a footing in the Academic Groves—if it takes place it will give to science a new *éclat* ! "

[2] Faraday, in 1815, wrote : " Of the fitness of their union—it might have been better for both had they never met ".

tinent with his wife and Faraday (who acted as secretary-valet) to investigate : and, though England and France were then at war, he (forestalling the League of Nations Committee for International Intellectual Co-operation) visited the enemy. French Savants received these two enemies of their country as friends, honouring them with the greatest distinctions.

What was the war to Davy and Faraday ? Their minds were just then on greater volcanos ! Science knew no boundaries—French and English Scientists were brothers, though their blood-brothers were fighting in rival armies.

A few years later Davy invented his safety-lamp,[1] by means of which, and ever after till the present day, miners were freed from the danger of introducing light into the mines. To the scientist this humane invention was a mere item—done *en passant*. Yet it caused a practical revolution in coal-mining !

His mind had gone on to researches in electro-magnetism—and during 1820-23 he

[1] Mr. Playfair, in 1816, wrote of the Safety Lamp : " (It) is a present from philosophy to the arts and to the class of men furthest removed from the influence of science. This is exactly such a case as we should choose to place before Bacon, were he to revisit the earth, in order to give him an idea of the advancement which philosophy has made since the time when he pointed out to her the route which she ought to pursue. . . . The result is as wonderful as it is important. . . . There is hardly in the whole compass of art or science a single invention of which we would rather be the author ".

made his results known to the Royal Society, of which he was then President.

Among his writings it is no surprise to find " Elements of Chemical Philosophy " *and* " Salmonia, or Days of Fly-fishing," for poetry in him had risen to philosophy on the one hand, and, on the other, he was still a truant! To him we owe the Zoological Gardens ; and the Science Museum at South Kensington arose from his ¬persistent representations to his fellow trustees of the British Museum.

His quest fulfilled, his Mission successful, his simple life was a merging of poetry in science, raising both, by mental pilgrimage, to philosophy, in an age when poets did not disdain to know something at least of their brothers, the scientists !

You see, in the very face of Sir Humphry Davy, the ever-present dreaming boy. What a beautiful face ![1] Fit for the poets' corner.

The Royal Institution made his way easy[2] —he had no tastes beyond the limits of his

---

[1] Ticknor said of him that at the age of 37 he had " all the freshness and bloom of 25 and (was) one of the handsomest men I have seen in England. He has a great deal of vivacity, talks rapidly, though with great precision, and is so much interested in conversation that his excitement amounts to nervous impatience and keeps him in constant motion ".

[2] Though his wife does not seem to have done as much, for in 1823 Davy wrote : " To add to my annoyances, I find my home as usual after the arrangements made by the mistress of it, without female servants—but in this world we have to suffer and bear, and from Socrates down to humble mortals, domestic discomfort seems a sort of philosophical fate ! "

purse. In an age when men threw their cares
on God, he sailed on untroubled seas, every
step of his work recognized as it went along.
When his assistant began to become a com-
petitor and aroused in him the jealousy natural
to mankind, he was in a position to check him.
As President of the R.S. he refused to acknow-
ledge the value of Faraday's first individual
discoveries.[1] He himself had never to battle
for recognition.[2] His was just a direct struggle
with nature, over which he was triumphantly
victorious—yet had he never sat by the river-
side in boyhood, waiting for a trout to rise,
and idly watching the gases that rise from
pools of water, the course of modern chemistry,
and therefore of modern industry, might have
been different : had Davy not won through
to the R.I., Faraday might never have been
able to develop *his* genius.

Is it Chance or Fate that plays this game
with mankind ?—or is there in it something
supernatural ordering this which to us seems
chance ?

How many other humble boys dream the
same dreams, have the same gifts as these

[1] It is remarkable to note that Bacon did not recognise, or
overlooked, Harvey's great discovery of the circulation of
the blood.

[2] Though in 1824 he wrote : " One might be induced to say,
why should I labour for public objects merely to meet abuse ?
I am irritated by them more than I ought to be ; but I am
getting wiser every day—recollecting Galileo and the times
when philosophers were burnt for their services ".

M

sons of handloom-weaver, wood-carver and blacksmith, who never set themselves the list of studies set himself by Davy, and to whom Fate never gives an opening ? All inborn genius does not come to fulfilment—many are lost by the way. Many quests fail, many missions are unfulfilled. Plenty of boys, we may be sure, over England at that time, started as Davy started, and arrived nowhere.

Davy never recovered from the shock of his mother's death; and soon after he had a slight attack of paralysis from which he eventually died.

Was there in him some peculiar balance of characteristics and of circumstances, or some balanced growth of ductless glands—which fitted him physically for his vocation as a fox-hound is fitted for fox-hunting ?

In such men there seems to be an inborn seed—and when this meets favourable soil it blooms.[1] There seem to be psychological moments in such lives when all things work towards fulfilment, and the cause of these moments—as Davy himself said : " *Has no abiding place, although its source is everlasting.*"

---

[1] It is worth noting that his mother, to whom he was devoted, had those qualities which were lacking in his father, and brought her five children through periods of financial disaster.

CHAPTER III

FARADAY

" *I have always loved science more than money . . .
I cannot afford to get rich* ".

M. FARADAY.

I HAVE seen in a tropical island, a little negro
boy, who runs errands for a chemist-shop,
sitting on the front step in the sunlight, poring
over a huge volume. It is the British *Pharma-
copœia* he reads, and he hopes to make a chemist of himself. Is it ambition or love of
learning, or both, that prompts him to this
lonely and dry study ? Will he make anything of it ? Who knows !

At the end of the eighteenth century a little
English boy who, a moment ago, was playing
marbles in the street with the children of the
neighbourhood,[1] could be seen sitting in the
back room of a bookbinder's shop in London,
his tools and materials pushed aside, the dank
smell of glue and leather in his nostrils, wasting
his master's time, obliviously deep in some
scientific book sent to be bound. What does
he make of it ? Who could dream this boy

[1] *Michael Faraday, His Life and Work*, by Sylvanus Thompson (Cassell, 1898).

171

would transform the entire world ? Only a year before he had been delivering newspapers,[1] calling out the news of the day at street corners. So well had he served his master that he was promoted to learn bookbinding.

This was a big step for him from the black-smith's forge of his father and brother, who lived round the corner in the mews. They were proud of him ; to have a bookbinder in the family was a lift-up indeed !

As a child, he had struck sparks from his father's anvil, and on sparks his life evolved. Beside the forge the love of God had been hammered into his soul, for his father was a " Glassite " or " Sandemanian," and he, with all his family, belonged to this Scottish Non-conformist sect (one arising from the spirit left over from the Levellers of Cromwell's Army) ; sturdily against established religion, inde-pendently persisting that every chapel should govern itself.

When he went home to the Mews at night, Michael joined in the family Bible-reading,[2] which went on all his life, strictly puritanical. He had one boy-friend to whom he confided his ideas of cold morality, from which he never afterwards swerved, and to this friend he confessed his love of natural science.

[1] *Michael Faraday*, by Randall (Leonard Parsons).
[2] Prof. Thompson says : " Faraday was able to erect an absolute barrier between his science and his religion "—but to me he was quite clearly a mystic.—A.D.

FARADAY

Metals were everywhere in this boy's early environment, and so he read all he could get hold of about their nature, fascinated by the marvels the books revealed.

One day he heard of some lectures to be given about chemistry. How he longed to go to them! But a shilling was the price of admission to each one, more than he could afford. He confided to his brother this longing, and the good fellow gave him the needed shillings.

Armed with pencil and note-book, Michael went along and made careful reports of all he heard.[1]

Before long he was handing on his new knowledge, in an ecstasy of delight, to a little circle of acquaintances formed by the youth who was his confidant. Who, seeing them, and hearing the self-taught lecturer, could have imagined that this boy would grow up to change the whole of physical science and the arts of civilized life?

One day there came into the bookbinder's back room a gentleman with volumes to be bound—he saw the beautiful-looking boy, so deep in a book that he never noticed this important customer. And, little by little,

[1] Among his notes found after his death, the following remark reveals his nature : " Do not many fail because they look rather to the renown to be acquired than to the pure acquisition of knowledge and the delight which the contented mind has in acquiring it for its own sake ".

finding him always studying, he began to question him. What was he reading ?

Science.

A blacksmith's son trying to teach himself Science ! Whatever for ?

Just because it fascinated him : just because he, too, had ideas about these things—why, no one knows. But chance played a winning card on him now.

The gentleman happened to be a member of the Royal Institution where Sir Humphrey Davy was making a stir with wonderful lectures ; and one day he took Michael Faraday with him to hear the famous scientist speak.

The eager youth sat there enthralled, of course, quite unnoticed, taking his painstaking notes. When an experiment was too difficult for him to understand, he put in his note-book : " Here I was unable to follow him," and passed on to the next one. He could understand quite a lot, for had he not made experiments himself, as far as his weekly pocket-money would allow ? Had he not himself already constructed an " electrical machine " and other scientific models, out of his own head, or by the help of the book-binder's clients' books, inspired by the lectures for which he had spent his brother's shillings ? It was second nature to him, lit by flashes of intuition which came out of nature and his dreaming mind. Spiritually inclined, he

thought trade " vicious and selfish," and longed
to escape from it into the " Service of
Science " which seemed to him " amiable and
liberal."

As he sat absorbed, watching Sir Humphrey
Davy, poet and natural philosopher, and fine
to look upon, then only thirty-four years old,
an inspired experimenter, Faraday felt an
affinity with him. But he dared not approach
him.

He went home with his notes, and, in a corner
of the Mews, by candle-light, he began that very
night to copy out and elaborate the notes he
had taken. Working on this at every odd
moment until it was complete, he then bound
it ; and he sent the volume, with its exquisite
penmanship and decorative lettering, to the
object of his hero-worship, and with a letter
asking for help in getting scientific occupation.

Then ; delivering it after hours by hand
himself, he walked away, elated and full of
youthful hope and dreams of freedom (even
though he had been snubbed when he had left
a similar letter at the Royal Society and had
been curtly told by the porter there was " no
reply "), his spirits rose again as he handed in
his book to Davy. His brother was now
preparing to be a gas-fitter, but he had already
gone further than that—why should he not hope
to work for the man he worshipped ?—what
the son of a woodcarver had done, the son of

a blacksmith might do too ? His ambition was just eagerness to get to his vocation.

Davy, touched by the gift from the unknown boy, asked Pepys what he could do about it.

" Do ? " said Mr. Pepys, " put him to wash bottles—you'll soon see what he's fit for."

On Christmas Eve, 1812, the youth had the first great thrill of his life—a letter actually came from his hero. An interview was arranged ; the first contact between two minds which together altered the whole course of the world's industry.

Davy advised him to stick to his trade, and even offered to get for him the binding of books for the Institution. Back he went to his father's smithy—depressed beyond words.

Then, one night, just as he was getting into bed, a carriage drew up at the Mews and a footman left a letter—for him ! His heart in his mouth, with flickering fingers he lit the candle, and opened it—could it be true ? The letter was from Davy, asking him to call to see him the following morning !

His imagination on fire, he dressed himself in his best and went to this rendezvous, as other boys go to their love-making ; and he came away engaged to keep the laboratory cleaner than the last apprentice had kept it. He was just twenty-one—and felt like a nobleman come into his inheritance ! The Institution

was to pay him 25/- a week and give him a
bed on the premises.

The next thing that happened was even
more thrilling, for Davy was making ready to
go abroad with his wife, and he took the
laboratory assistant with him as secretary and
valet. Throughout this tour the young man,
so meticulous, such a puritan, kept a journal ;
the foreign trip was to him what a University
is to other men.

His chief excitements were in Florence, when
he saw first Galileo's first telescope, and then
" the grand experiment of burning a diamond ":
at Rome where experiments were made on the
magnetization of a needle by the rays of the
sun; and when he met Volta in Naples. A
very serious young man on a very serious
journey.

But he was happiest of all to be back in
Albemarle Street again, washing bottles and
watching experiments, too busy with his own
notes at night to even think of reading Scott,
or of going to see Mrs. Siddons at Drury Lane.

His salary had now been raised to 30/- a
week, he was in Heaven !

All around him wonders were going on ;
and he began to get into direct touch with
others working to the same ends. He wrote
in his note-book : " Truth should be his
primary object "—religion in his science all the
way along. His relaxation was to go home to

the Mews, to watch his father at the well-known forge, to take part in the Bible-readings in the chapel.

This exemplary fellow thought Love " the pest and plague of human life—the curse that often brings a wife ! " In the middle ages he would have been a monk.

He began writing articles and succeeded in getting them published, and, in his spare time he constructed the first electric motor (1821). This was his great romance !

But in the Sandemanian church he met the daughter of a working silversmith (metals seemed to mark his fate) and after a time decided, quite prosaically, that he would like to marry her. His love-letter to her, in the first lines of which he said, " I am so tired," ended : " As I ponder and think of you, chlorides, trials, oils, Davy, steel, miscellanea, mercury, and fifty other professional fancies swim before and drive me farther and farther into the quandary of stupidness ! "

Was there ever a stranger wooing ? Yet she was won by it. They married in the same year that he made his motor. A red letter year for him !

Had his obedient wife only known, she ought to have aroused him from his " stupidness," for even then he was showing signs of the overwork and over-specialization that was to bring him in his old age to senile decay.

Before long he was in Davy's place at the
Institution, not working for humanity, or even
for worldly success—the world closed down,
leaving him in his cell, with his metals and his
motors, his chemistry. But had he been a monk,
at work in a monastery, his hours would
have been better ordered—his horizon wider.

*Yet this is one of the Fathers of Modern
Civilization.* The history of our industrial age
divides itself into " before—and after—Faraday," for we no longer think in terms of the
Stone age and the Iron Age. This is the Age
of Electricity, he its foremost founder. He
and those who came after him have given us
greater freedom than ever Rousseau thought
of ! Altering the pace of life, bringing the
ends of the earth near, to speak and even to see
across space—to draw music from the air,
giving us light to see by, giving us power to
move mighty machines, to fly in the upper
air ! Even power to heal and prevent
disease ; and to milk cows, wash clothes—
without hands ; even to call forth colour without paint or chemicals !

How did all this come about ?

Electro-chemistry was first put on a firm
basis by Sir Humphrey Davy ; but it was
Faraday who in 1834 first explained its true
laws, and later made its use in daily life prac-
ticable. Who would then have imagined its
uses to-day ; or that it would be applied, for

instance, even to purifying sewage! Still
less who would dream that the mysterious and
fascinating facts of chemical affinity might be
explained as a form of electrical action?

Science is ever passing through veritable
re-births. Electricity was known long ago,
and was demonstrated before Queen Elizabeth
in the time of Bacon by Dr. William Gilbert
of Colchester (1540–1603); so though the
Greeks knew a little about it, it really started
in England in the 16th century. But all this
was little more than a study of frictional
electricity and of magnetism.

Still, it paved the way for experiments
which through Franklin, Ampère, Dalton and
Davy, culminated with Faraday.

By the eighteenth century, thanks to Boyle,
Newton and Gray, to Von Guericke and du Fay,
it was proved that all materials could be more
or less electrified by friction; but it was
Franklin, in America, who defined the " posi-
tive " and " negative " character of differently
electrified bodies.

Quite early in the century of Faraday's birth
electric machines were designed which could
produce a spark, and also a shock : and, before
that, the Leyden Jar, or condenser, had been
made, following a discovery of Von Guericke's
a hundred years or so previously. It was
Franklin who identified lighting with the
electric spark.

All this and more was preliminary—but it was not till 1835 when Faraday enunciated his Law of Electrolysis, that real progress began. He had revolutionized electric theory; and all modern electrical invention is based on Faraday's work on electro-magnetism, which was even more important than his theory of electrolysis, shewing the path to modern dynamo-electric machinery.

Do you say there is no idealism, there is nothing spiritual, in all this? It is the very root of modern industry. Electricity, in all its forms, is an increasingly paying concern. Yet, though he might have easily made thousands a year as a technical consultant, Faraday steadily refused to do so.

His reason for refusing to make money was as simple as everything else about him. To bring himself to get rich meant loss of freedom, and his life's game depended on having time and liberty for it. At the outset, and as long as he wanted it, he had a good home at the Royal Institute, and later a house at Hampton Court given him by the Queen; his wife, to whom he remained quite prosaically devoted, had all she wanted, and they had no children to provide for. The Institution, too, made his experiments possible and gave him in return for certain work there, the little cash he needed.

That there is an element of philosophy in

both electricity and chemistry, few people realize.

This man was in religion as believing as a child ; all his knowledge never disturbed his Faith. " I do believe," he wiote, " from the bottom of my heart, that Christ is with us."

Why did the spirit of enquiry enter into this son of a God-fearing blacksmith ?

Why did he apprentice himself to a bookbinder ?

Why not a harness-maker ?

Was it chance, or choice ?

Had he been apprenticed to a harness-maker it is likely the hole course of events might have been different !

Fate had a hand in it, for the bookbinder's shop was nearby. Yet Faraday was led by intuition all his life.[1] He combined the faculties of an " intuitional " and an " intellectual." He was all his life like an inspired child. Though he valued his wife, the greatest emotions in his life were for his work and for his God ; although he wrote to Mrs. Faraday : " Nothing rests me so much as communion with you." His natural place was the mon-

[1] (a) Prof. Thompson says of him : Often a discovery arose from some chance or trivial incident transmuted by his " lateral vision ".

(b) Von Helmholtz wrote of him : " With quite wonderful sagacity and intellectual precision Faraday performed in his brain the work of a great mathematician without using a single mathematical formula.   He saw with the mind's eye— this was the part of his path where so few could follow him ".

astery of science, and almost like a mediæval
monk he lived in the Institution where he now
stands in pure white marble—a saintly, un-
forgettable figure !

For politics he cared nothing, he had no
outside interests.

Though accepting as time went on many
honours which were pressed on him, he refused
the Presidency of the Royal Society and the
Chair of Chemistry in London University, and
the Vice-Presidency of the Albert Hall. When
advising various Government departments he
declined a fee.[1] He even declined a pension.
But he said, "A Government should for its
own sake honour the men who do honour
and service to the country . . . not by
indiscriminate knighthoods and baronetcies,
but by recognizing scientific people as a
class."

Now wherever you have the combination
of deeply religious love of God with passionately enquiring love of nature, you get an
unusual personality which chance and circumstance may develop in a variety of ways. He
vowed : " Not to despise small beginnings "
and insisted on " a continual comparison of
the small and the great . . . for (he said) the
small often contains the great in principle as

---

[1] It was Faraday's pleading with the Royal Commissioners
of the Public Schools that eventually caused the introduction
of Science into the school curricula. His educational ideas
were far in advance of his time.

the great does the small . . . thus the mind becomes comprehensive."

Instinct, flashes of intuition, led him to follow investigations and open paths still being followed even now. Intuition and persistence made him one of the most brilliant experimenters ever known. The very words he coined are in use to-day ; and these words he used, whenever possible, instead of notations because he was not very fond of mathematics.[1]

History is rhythmic, progress is cumulative ; endless beginnings are made, and at the psychological moment the work of all the precursors culminates in the mind of one man— Faraday thus supplied the missing link. If asked how he made his grand discovery, he could only reply, " By intuition."

He had a brain-wave one day—an idea occurred to him, and for years afterwards he tried to make this idea come true—to make his obsession real. In the midst of much other work he played with his great idea— but for years and years in vain. What he believed, he could not prove—the thing would not work.

He was, in this, a visionary.

"*He saw in his mind's eye, the lines of force passing through the air from the magnet.*"[2] He

---

[1] Prof. Thompson says : " He had little sympathy with either text-book science or with mere examinations ".
[2] Wilfred L. Randell, *Michael Faraday.*

184

visualized things which had never been known.

At last,[1] his wire charged with electricity for the first time revolved round the pole of his magnet ![2] This staid nonconformist danced round the table, in the presence of his sanctimonious brother-in-law, shouting : "There they go ! There they go ! We have succeeded at last ! " and went off to the Theatre ! Too excited to stay at home ! He was at one moment like an inspired child—at another like a Roundhead unbending after a victory !

" I believe," he once wrote, " that the truth of the future cannot be brought to (man's) knowledge by any exertion of his mental powers, however exalted they may be ; that it is made known to him by other teaching than his own . . . as if man by reasoning could find out God ! "

Life went normally on until ten years after his great experiment had first worked. The results of his busy concentration showed themselves. His memory began to fail him. He was temporarily " finished." He had overlooked his own bodily machine and had transgressed laws which had never interested him. In time he regained control enough to go on for another ten years of restless analysis, but now, bothered by his memory, which often gave

[1] 1831.
[2] Faraday amused and delighted his audience at one of his lectures by throwing a scuttle of coals and a poker at the magnet, to which they clung !

out, the child in him found vent in the making of a " Flower-book "[1]—pressed flowers and grasses beautifully arranged, which, at the age of 59, he made for his wife ! Could anything have been more Wordsworthian ? Like Wordsworth, he kept in sympathy with children. Remembering his own boyhood, he started, at the Royal Institute, the now famous " Children's Xmas Lectures." For a hundred years the eager faces of little boys electrified by the excitement of really seeing how things work, have proved how well he understood the need there is in boyhood for an approach to the mysteries of nature.

He himself talked to them on everything—on the contents of the breakfast table, or the chemistry of a candle.

But well though he remembered his own boyhood, one experience of early manhood was not forgotten later on.

When he was thirty-three he had been elected F.R.S., and this estranged him from Davy—who had actively opposed his election, and who even wanted to get the credit for work done by his assistant while he was out of Town ! This jealousy in so beautiful a personality as his hero, Davy, must have left its mark on Faraday—himself an almost too perfect character. Yet in his turn he " attributed the invention of the electro-magnet to Moll and

[1] Preserved in the R.I.

186

FARADAY

Henry, whose work was frankly based on Sturgeon's."[1]

Sturgeon had for years been doing pioneer work in electro-magnetism and Faraday persistently ignored him! Curious, how even so great a mind can close in upon itself.

It is believed that senility never comes to clean lives when the mind has been used to its fullest extent—yet this man, when not much over seventy, fell into second childhood, satisfied to be wheeled in a chair to the window, to watch the people going to chapel!

And, tired of that, he closed in still more upon himself till he took no notice of the people around him. His life was a triumph; was his death perhaps symbolic of too much Puritanism and of over-specialization? Yet in specializing he took a broad view for it was he who, a friend of Turner, really brought about the French Impressionism which changed all Art, for he persistently impressed upon his artist friends the necessity for experimenting with colour for themselves.

" His work," cried Tyndall, " excites admiration, but contact with him warms and elevates the heart; here is surely a strong man."

[1] *Michael Faraday*, by Sylvanus Thompson.

BIBLIOGRAPHY

The Life and Work of Sir Jagadis Chunder Bose,
F.R.S., by Patrick Geddes. Longmans.
The Voice of Life. Pamphlet, by Sir Jagadis Chunder
Bose, F.R.S.
Plant Autographs and their Revelations, by Sir Jagadis
Chunder Bose. Longmans.
The Web of Indian Life, by Sister Nivedita. Long-
mans.
Mother India, by Kathleen Mayo. Cape.
Cities in Evolution, by Patrick Geddes. Williams and
Norgate.
The Interpreter: Geddes, the Man and His Gospel,
by Amelia Defries. Geo. Routledge and Sons.
Report to the Durbar of Indore, by Patrick Geddes.
Batsford.
Pillars of Society, by Gardner. Nisbet.
St. Columba, by Victor Branford. P. Geddes and
Colleagues.
Our Social Inheritance, by Geddes and Branford.
LePlay House Press, 65 Belgrave Road, S.W.1.
The Drift to Revolution, by Victor Branford. LePlay
House Press.
The Banker's Part in
Reconstruction   ,,   ,,   ,,
Interpretations and
Forecasts   ,,   ,,   ,, Duckworth.
Address, by Nicholas Roerich.
A Conference of Pleasure, by Sir Francis Bacon. Edited
by James Spedding. 1870.
Francis Bacon, by Israel Levine. Leonard Parsons.
Humphrey Davy, by T. E. Thorpe, F.R.S. Cassell.
History of Chemistry, by T. E. Thorpe. Watts.

BIBLIOGRAPHY

Michael Faraday: His Life and Work, by Sylvanus Thompson, F.R.S. Cassell. 1898.
Michael Faraday, by W. I. Randall. Leonard Parsons.
The Book of the Art of Cennino Cennini (approx. 1398). Translated by C. S. Herringham. George Allen and Unwin.

The author is grateful to the above-named publishers for permission to quote from the books issued by them ; and to the Secretary and the Librarian of the Royal Institution of Great Britain for their kindness in checking the facts in Chapters II and III, Part 2. Also to *The Illustrated London News* for certain of the illustrations.